10/6

Major Major

Major Major

Memories of an Older Brother

Terry Major-Ball

with an Introduction by
James Hughes-Onslow

Duckworth

First published in 1994 by
Gerald Duckworth & Co. Ltd.
The Old Piano Factory
48 Hoxton Square, London N1 6PB
Tel: 071 729 5986
Fax: 071 729 0015

A catalogue record for this book is available
from the British Library

ISBN 0 7156 2631 0

The author and publishers are grateful to Associated
Newspapers (*Evening Standard, Daily Mail* and *Mail
on Sunday*) for permission to reproduce press
photographs, and to the *Independent* for the
photograph of the author and his sister
(Plate 23; photo: Herbie Knott).

Typeset by Ray Davies
Printed and bound in Great Britain by
Biddles Ltd., Guildford and King's Lynn

Contents

To my family

Plates

11. John Major and some Major's Garden Ornaments in Burton Road.
    Grandmother Milly with Fiona at home in Thornton Heath.
    John feeding pills to the hamster, Christine.
12. John and Norma's wedding, photographed by Terry.
13. John Major as Chairman of the Housing Committee at Lambeth Council.
14 & 15. Holidays at Butlins.
16 & 17. Family homes.
18. Terry and Shirley with the Beverley Sisters.
    Terry with trainees at Zippo's Circus.
19. Zippo's Circus.
20 & 21. Trip to New York, November 1993.
22. Terry and Shirley outside their house in Wallington.
23. American roots: John Major with Bill Clinton in Pittsburgh.
    Terry with his sister Pat.
24. Terry in Wallington.
    John and Terry at Terry's house in January 1994.

Acknowledgments

First I must thank my wife Shirley for putting up with me researching and writing this book and answering the enquiries of journalists when in her view there were more important jobs to be done around the house. Thank you, too, to my sister Pat who has taken the trouble to come to my house and read all the manuscripts and help with ideas, family memories and photographs. My brother John and sister-in-law Norma have also been on the end of a telephone to encourage me and answer my questions but I must emphasise that they have not seen this book, so cannot be blamed for its contents.

Cal McCrystal of the *Independent* was helpful in sparking my enthusiasm for starting this project, and he has been one of the few newspaper men to take the trouble to report me accurately. Thank you to the staff at the Colindale newspaper library and to journalists at *The Stage* for their courteous assistance.

Christina Hughes-Onslow has allowed James to work at weekends, nights and holidays helping me by editing the book, despite the demands of four small children. We have had valuable support from Andrew Wilson, *Evening Standard* literary editor, Angus McGill, who suggested the title *Major Major*, Tricia Phillips who organised the New York trip and the ever eager team on Londoner's Diary who seem obsessed with everything I do.

My thanks to Mrs Menna Williams, Mr Goodman, Mrs McKeen, Mrs Rowley, Mr Chapman, Mrs Tong, Mrs West, Miss Janet Smith, Ruth Bagley, Mr Latimer, Mrs Fox, Mr Hore, Mr Carr, Mr Hayes, Mr Revill, Mrs Gould, Claire Harrington, Mrs Onions, Mr Yeardley, Mr Freeman, and all the other Superintendent Registrars, Registrars and Archivists who have helped me with my enquiries. A special mention must go to Mr Bond with whom I worked so well over a long distance, to Mr Horne and the St Catherine's House staff, and to Dizzy who I believe is no longer with us. I must not forget the librarians especially those of the Guildhall Library, Sutton Library, Westminster Library, Croydon Library and the New York City Library.

My thanks to Valda Davis of Walsall Swimming Club, who helped with so much information, Mrs Mitton of the Lock Museum and Dorothy Williams and friends from Smithwick with whom I spent such a nice day when they came to London. Thank you Mrs Arbon from Gainsborough and fellow Delvers (a local history society) for providing information about the dancing school there, with a video and a book. I would like to thank Mr Dodd of British Telecom for his help in tracing old telephone records and Miss M. Boyle of the City Varieties, Max Tyler, David Drummond and Martin Burton for help with the theatre and the circus. Thank you to Debra Aspen at Virgin Atlantic and all the Virgin ladies.

Finally thanks to all my old neighbours and friends in Worcester Park for remembering my parents. People like Mrs Cowley, her sons and daughter, Phyllis Swain, Mrs Weallan and her daughter, Mrs Scot and both her daughters, John Carey and Eddie Scammell.

Many other people have helped my research and I would like to thank them all and to apologise to anyone I have failed to mention.

Introduction

by James Hughes-Onslow

I first met Terry and Shirley Major-Ball in June 1991 when they came to the Myatt's Fields Fair, held in a small park about 100 yards from Burton Road where the Prime Minister's family used to live during the 1960s. This park between Brixton Road and Coldharbour Lane used to contain watercress and strawberry beds and is still an oasis in the inner city council estates of Brixton. The fair is like a country fête with garden stalls and tombolas, except that the local church, St James's, where Terry's and John's sister Pat was married, is now a Black Roof Housing Association project. It is just opposite Templar Street, where John lived when he first became a Lambeth councillor in 1968. It was here that John met Marcus Lipton, Labour MP for Lambeth who first took John to the House of Commons.

I already knew Terry from long telephone calls from the *Evening Standard*, clarifying such important matters as what the Prime Minister likes for breakfast, or whether he prefers rugger or soccer, and I had explained to him that I lived in Myatt's Fields. Terry and Shirley came to lunch with us on the day of the fair and Terry complained that the area was not what it was in his day. People did not clear up their rubbish or keep their front gardens tidy. He had a steady stream of family anecdotes which lasted from the time he arrived at noon until about 7.30pm when our children were in the bath and he asked to be taken to Brixton to catch the bus back to Croydon. When I said he should be writing all these stories down

11

to correct some of the wilder stories in the newspapers Terry told me he was already at work on this, making frequent visits to the newspaper library at Colindale in north London to look up references to his father's days in the theatre and the circus.

Terry showed me what he had written when we went to New York together in November 1993. It was just like Terry, full of family history and political philosophy told as only he could do it, but not as structured as a publisher would require. He asked me to help him polish it up and find a publisher. Sometimes I have gone too far and he has sent my suggestions back to me, saying that he doesn't like them or they aren't quite like him, or that I've got some facts wrong. But on one occasion he complimented me by saying I had cracked his writing style and, after consultation with his sister Pat, he had very few alterations to make. Terry is always very meticulous with his facts, especially after he was quoted in a tube advertisement for the *Evening Standard* saying his book was unlike all other political biographies in that it contained nothing but the truth.

It came as a shock to read, while we were working on this, the *Daily Telegraph* gossip columnist Quentin Letts saying that we were unable to find a publisher because all publishers had turned it down. He quoted one publisher as saying that the book was more Pooterish than Pooter. One expects gossip columnists to get things wrong but not so completely wrong. In *The Diary of a Nobody* Mr Pooter is a dreary, colourless, rather pretentious little man, with an elaborate notion of his own position in society's pecking order. This book is just as illuminating about life in the suburbs of London, but Terry is a very different character. One wonders whether the publisher who allegedly said this had bothered to read even the two chapters which had been written at that time. Terry is one of those rare people who actually addresses everyone he meets as if they were his equals, without trying to assess how important they are or whether they are going to be any use to him.

When I went to New York with Terry I found he addressed Wall Street bankers and men working in the streets in exactly the same way. In computer terminology there is an expression to describe the system in which the typeface and format that comes out on your printer is exactly as you see it on the screen. It is called Wysiwyg, or What You See Is What You Get. Terry is Wysiwyg. One sometimes wonders whether this is deliberate or whether it is ingrained in his character, but either way it is entirely commendable. It is probably a legacy of his father who worked in the circus, a community in which everyone is obliged to help, even with the most mundane tasks. Not many people can do that, but more people should try it.

The sniggering classes will snigger at this book. They always find references to garden gnomes, circus clowns and trapeze artists immensely funny. It is strange that although the Prime Minister's critics have questioned many aspects of his family history they never doubted that his father was a trapeze artist, even though there are very few facts to bear this out. At that time Tom Major used a stage name which no one even knows, so it is impossible to check his trapeze career, but pictures of the Prime Minister's father balancing on a high wire have proved so irresistible to cartoonists and headline writers that no one is prepared to doubt them. Mercifully it is a free country, so that if readers want to laugh that is a matter for them. They may be moved to cry when they find a family that has struggled in a very resourceful way against great difficulties without ever being a burden on others. They will see how Terry and his sister Pat held the family together and paid the rent while John was still at school and while both parents were ill and unable to earn a living. It is no wonder the Prime Minister speaks of family values and has such a close relationship with his own family. He is well aware of the debt he owes them.

Those who read this book will never again be able to describe the Prime Minister as a grey man. In an era when too few politicians have any experience of life outside politics we have a Prime Minister who comes from a more colourful background than any of his predecessors at No 10 Downing Street. If Terry succeeds in putting the record straight on that, all his hard work will have been worthwhile.

1

Young John, Prime Minister

The night before my younger brother John became leader of the Tory party in November 1990 I was at No 11 Downing Street, then of course his official residence as Chancellor of the Exchequer, sitting in the kitchen with my sister-in-law Norma. I was to play only a small part in the unfolding drama. I was there just to show family support. This was after all the day of the politician, surrounded as John was by enthusiastic supporters and advisers.

As Norma had come up to London from Huntingdon that day and hadn't had time to buy anything, there wasn't much food in the house. Between us we had eaten what little there was when Graham Bright, a member of John's campaign team, arrived with the latest figures of support, indicating that things were going well.

Then quite late John came in, looking tired but in pretty good shape considering the circumstances. Norma asked if he would like a cup of tea, which was about all she had to offer.

'Yes, please,' he said. 'And I wouldn't mind something to eat.'

It seemed strange to me that throughout the day no one had thought of asking the Chancellor whether he would like something to eat, and I must say I felt a little sheepish, having helped to demolish what was left in his fridge.

For me it was a kind of role reversal. Thirty years before when John and I had worked together in the garden ornament business in Camberwell, often too busy to stop for meals, it was John who went to the baker's for cakes or buns. I had to stay to answer the telephone and John was fleeter of foot than I was. Well I remember the day he had to scale the seven-foot wall to fetch some food because the gates were boarded up after a lorry had backed into them in the night. He was brought back by a policeman who asked me sternly whether I knew the young man, and it was really only our matching cement-stained clothing which allayed his suspicion, as I recount later.

This time, however, it was clearly my responsibility. I asked John what he wanted.

'Anything,' he said, just as he always did in the old days. 'Pie and chips if they have them.'

Camberwell is one thing, but where do you find a pie and chips near Downing Street? John's driver told me there was a place nearby but said it was nearly closing time. So I gave him a fiver and he did the rest. I ordered some chips for myself, and John and I ate together in the kitchen.

It was the last time I saw him at No 11 before he was elected Tory leader. The next time I was there, a few days later at the weekend, I remember I was talking to John when Jeffrey Archer came through the passage from No 10, saying he had just seen Sir Denis pacing around next door while Mrs Thatcher was upstairs packing.

I shall never forget the evening of the leadership election. I was at home in Wallington, near Croydon in south London, and not in Downing Street – which was probably just as well because it was an emotional occasion and I'm not sure that I could have handled large numbers of people. My wife Shirley, daughter Fiona and son Mark, both in their 20s but still living at home, hadn't yet returned from work. I was sitting on the settee waiting for the result, just as I imagine many other people were throughout the country.

Tense as I was, I found it strangely amusing to hear commentators and MPs desperately filling in time by assuring me in almost conspiratorial asides about things I knew already. Michael Dobbs said that, far from being a grey man, John's private personality was witty, humorous and very incisive. Thank you Michael, you are quite right, I felt like saying, but how many people would believe this coming from a master of fictional political intrigue? Emma Nicholson mentioned Mrs Thatcher's now famous back-seat driver remark, asking: 'Do we want to be left with her in the back seat, and her favourite nominee in the front?' Ian Lang, however, said the new Prime Minister would be very much his own man and spoke of the now famous dinner when John first attracted Mrs Thatcher's attention by getting the better of her in an argument.

All these things and much more I knew for myself. No one who had known John as long as I had, through some very difficult times, could doubt his toughness and determination to get on. But I did wonder how convincing these people sounded to the rest of the country.

When the Chairman of the 1922 Committee, Cranley Onslow, emerged from Committee Room 12 with the votes cast – 131 for Michael Heseltine, 56 for Douglas Hurd and 185 for John Major – a loud gasp came over the television and an even louder one from me on my settee. John had missed an outright win by two votes. I was living the drama as though I were part of it.

Almost immediately, it seemed, Michael Heseltine was on the screen saying he wouldn't be standing in the next round and urging MPs to vote for John. Soon Douglas Hurd was saying that John Major was the right leader to restore unity to the party. 'I shall vote for him in the third ballot,' he said. 'I know he will be an excellent Prime Minister and he will have my full and unreserved support.'

By this time the commentators were delving further with their snippets of information about John, the new Tory leader and tomorrow the Prime Minister, telling us that he would be the youngest since Robert Peel in the 1840s.

I still find it impossible to describe my feelings at this point.

There I was, sitting on my settee, a tear in the corner of each eye, muttering 'Good luck, John', and 'So young John's the new Prime Minister', trying out the words to see how they sounded to my own incredulous ears as if I were taking part in the studio discussion that appeared to be taking place in my living-room or perhaps addressing our proud but long-dead parents.

Then John and Norma, both calm and collected and in a much less emotional state than I, appeared on my screen, standing outside No 11 Downing Street which had become so familiar to me. John praised Margaret Thatcher as one of the Conservative Party's great leaders. I was glad he did that. For me as for many of her admirers it was sad to know that the time seemed to have come for her to go, much though I felt, as I had done for a year or so, that she had to go for the sake of the party. I shed a tear for her too. John next thanked Michael Heseltine and Douglas Hurd for the way they had conducted their campaigns, standing down to avoid a third ballot. He already looked and sounded like a Prime Minister.

Then Andrew Roth, a writer of political profiles, appeared on the screen and made some very inaccurate remarks about my father. I suppose if you are in the thick of the fray like John you don't worry about such things, or at least you learn not to, but when you are quietly sitting in your suburban home without ever having been involved in public life and a man who has never spoken to you is there on television uttering dubious statements about your family, some of them rather hurtful, it stings. A badly researched article published at the time of John's first Budget as Chancellor had already made me realise that I should investigate the facts about my family. A well-known journalist had even suggested that I should write a book. Roth's remarks were to provide the necessary spur.

By way of telling us that John was not really working-class at all, or classless, as had been claimed in the leadership campaign, Roth said that Father had been a middle-class entrepreneur with several business failures to his name. This instantly touched a nerve with me because the only business my father had run was Major's Garden Ornaments, in which I had worked for many years of my life, as had my mother, my elder sister Pat and, to a lesser extent because he was much younger, my brother John.

Father's garden ornament venture was the only business he started after he left the stage. It is true that he tried working for a couple of firms, in one case as a bulk-coal agent, before starting out on his own. He looked at various options but settled for garden ornaments, having made some by hand many years previously. Starting with very little capital, he devised commercial ways of making and selling them, not an easy task in the difficult economic climate of the 1930s.

True, the business eventually collapsed, so that we had to sell our house, but this resulted from a bizarre combination of the Second World War, Father's declining health and a woman who tried to buy the firm without thinking her plans through properly. When she changed her mind and cancelled the deal, Father might have claimed compensation. If his health had been better and the family had been less principled, our history might have followed a very different path.

Andrew Roth went on to explain that Father was originally Tom Ball, but called himself Tom Major when he was a trapeze artist and later changed it to the grander-sounding Tom Major-Ball when he became an actor manager. How could John Major, who by rights (he said) should have a double-barrelled name, possibly claim to be classless? Could he have become Prime Minister if he had been called John Major-Ball?

This sounds very grand and clever, but alas once again Mr Roth had got most of his facts wrong. Yes, Father was originally called Ball, but the name he used during his short trapeze career is not recorded. As an actor-manager he called himself Tom Major, but the name Major-Ball was not used until after he left the stage.

As I hope this book shows, Father really did treat everyone as his equal, meeting in the course of a varied life an astonishing diversity of people from many parts of the world. It is an attitude of mind he successfully passed on to his children. How much better it would have been if Roth had been more thorough in his research.

When my son and daughter came home from work, Mark from Bourjois and Fiona from the Chanel office, both in Wallington, neither of them had heard the news. They later went out in Fiona's car, which didn't have a radio at the time, to go shopping and came back later in the evening. Reporters outside our front door who surged forward to ask them what they thought about their uncle's new job were astonished to be told quite truthfully that they knew nothing about it. Mark and Fiona found me quite exhausted by my afternoon as a lounge lizard, part elated by John's success, part furious about the inaccurate things Roth had been saying about Father.

Then my wife Shirley came home from the Whirlpool offices in Croydon, and she too told me about the reporters outside.

'They want you to go out and talk to them,' she said.

'Yes, I know they do,' I said, by now sounding more tetchy than exhilarated, scarcely extending to my family the welcome I would like to have done on this momentous evening. 'But I don't know what to say to them. I've never even met a reporter.'

Nothing could have been a starker contrast to John's and Norma's polished performance on the steps of No 10 a few minutes earlier. Behind that modest facade in Godalming Avenue I have to say that confusion reigned, as no doubt it does in Downing Street at times of crisis. There were constant ringings and knockings and thumps at the door, and Shirley bravely answered them all, fending them off surprisingly politely.

I think there is the making of a politician lurking there in my

Shirl. Much as I admire politicians for coping with the intrusions of the press, I suppose Prime Ministers have people to do this kind of work for them, keeping the press at bay, possibly even advising them what to say. But there we were, novice swimmers in at the deep end, trying to decide what to say, if anything, to a breed of human being I had not encountered before and who, according to one of their own, possess rat-like cunning.

It was Shirley who dented this stereotype, saying after peering out of the door into the darkness that she had seen a nice young lady from ITN.

'She's shivering, she looks quite frozen,' Shirley reported. 'And she has been told she can't go away until she has a quote from you.'

Though I tried to resist, Shirley knew she had hit my weak spot, a suffering female. Call me old-fashioned, but I can't decline an opportunity to help a young lady in trouble.

So I opened the door, and out I went, stepping into such a powerful beam of light that I could see nothing. It felt as if I were on stage, not standing outside my front door in Wallington.

A disembodied voice came out of the blackness beyond the source of the light as several other flashes went off in my face: Would I make a statement?

I was still feeling very emotional and strange. I had wanted John to win and expected him to, but I could still hardly believe that my brother – young John whom I used to push in his pram – was already as good as Prime Minister. I suppose I was almost in a state of shock, and although not ashamed to be proud of his achievement, thinking particularly how our parents would have felt if they had been alive at this moment, I was trying to appear calm and in control of events, as John always does, when in fact this was far from the case.

After I had uttered a few probably rather incoherent words, Shirley wisely guided me back inside where, with this ordeal over, I felt much better. I had almost recovered my equilibrium back on cloud nine, proud of the family in general as much as of John himself, when News at Ten came on. My own interview came over as a two-minute clip. It was a disaster. My face looked bloated, and I seemed drunk. What on earth can people have thought? In fact I hadn't consumed anything stronger than a cup of tea. It was a useful lesson to me that you can't be too careful with the media dragon.

(I do have one alcoholic reminder of that day in the shape of a bottle of champagne, which still remains unopened, left on the doorstep in a bag by the reporter from *The Sun*. Fiona picked it up when she returned from her evening out. The man later rang to ask for an interview – suggesting, perhaps on the strength of the News at Ten interview, that we meet in the pub. How could I refuse? It was to be my first visit to a pub in nearly ten years and I had a pint of shandy.)

I rang 10 Downing Street at about eleven that night to congratulate John. I was told he was busy, which didn't surprise me, but that he would be told I had called. Within a couple of minutes he called me back, as he always did and as I have subsequently discovered he still does if I don't get straight through. He sounded just the same John.

John becoming Prime Minister was obviously not going to affect our relationship. He was pleased but not exactly jumping up and down, or over-excited. After all he has been in politics a long time and knows the ups and downs of this business. He has a steady nerve. Mercifully there was no mention of my appearance on ITN half an hour earlier. I regret to say that I can't remember what we said to one another though I've tried to. Nor can he – I have since asked him for the purposes of this book.

Shirley lays even money that what I said was: 'Nice one, John. Mum and Dad would be proud of you.' She says this is what I'm always saying to him. In a way, it's what I hope I said to the Prime Minister designate – pretty banal I guess, but not too pompous.

Since he became Prime Minister he hasn't changed in any way in his attitude to me, though sometimes he can be very difficult to get hold of because of work.

Next morning I had hoped for a period of quiet reflection on the events of the previous day, but almost as soon as Shirley, Mark and Fiona had gone to work the press began to re-appear. In our quiet neighbourhood you know the cars that live there and the ones that are just visiting. Now there were numerous strange cars, some of them with their drivers still sitting in them. There were people in the road just hanging around, something you don't do lightly on a late November day. The door bell began to ring and then the telephone. Soon they never stopped.

What to do? I realised I had the advantage in that I knew they were there but they didn't know whether I was in the house or not. Or at least I *thought* I had the advantage. Perhaps they had been watching all night. Maybe they had spoken to my family when they left the house earlier. In any event I decided to keep out of sight, even when the reporters were banging loudly on the door. I simply wasn't prepared to risk repeating my performance on the News at Ten, especially as Shirley wasn't there to pull me in again.

I did go upstairs, however, and standing back from the window I could see them through the net curtains. Some were listening to car radios and using their car phones. Was it my number they were ringing? Some were in little groups talking, but there was a solitary figure on the far corner watching to see that I didn't slip out (or slip in?) by the the back way. I wondered whether Downing Street was so comprehensively covered.

Downstairs, where I was trying to work on my computer, I was constantly interrupted by the ringing of the telephone and the door bell, and the banging went on and on. After a while I developed a system of working through the quiet patches and then putting my hands over my ears and watching television when the telephone started up again. It was distracting to think it might be my wife, maybe even my brother, ringing to see how I was coping.

I became very concerned about the cost to newspapers and television companies of keeping all these reporters, photographers and cameramen outside my house. What on earth could I say that would justify the expense? Perhaps they were lured solely by the prospect of seeing me make a fool of myself, as I felt I might have done the previous night.

Anyway it seemed to me from watching the television, that there was enough going on elsewhere for them to report. I saw Margaret Thatcher go the Palace to see the Queen for the last time as Prime Minister. How she must have wished she could have slipped out by the garden back door, as I believe Lord Home did when he lost the 1964 election, and as I was beginning to hope I would one day be able to escape from my own home.

Once again I had to dab my eyes, because I felt for her. Though I believed, as I still do, that it was her own fault that she was out of office, it was desperately sad to see her go the way she did.

Then I saw John's car sweeping through the Palace gates, later returning to Downing Street with him as the new Prime Minister. Although I wasn't in a state of semi-shock, as I think I had been the previous evening, I still experienced a complex mixture of pride and nostalgia as I thought of all that my mother and father had been through in their lives.

Then Mark came home for a quick lunch break, bringing a friend. They had to run the gauntlet of the media men before and afterwards. We hardly had time to talk. On their way out the reporters gave chase as they ran down the road, asking them questions and taking pictures on the way. It was enough to persuade me that I was better off inside. Some of the reporters hung around until seven o'clock that night. David Gardner, a very nice man from the *Daily Mail*, a real gentleman according to Shirley who spoke to him several times that day, was the last to go.

1. Young John, Prime Minister

Next morning there were still some unfamiliar cars outside, so I remained out of sight. The telephone kept ringing, and on one occasion I counted two hundred rings before it gave up. It was all becoming rather a bore, so I rang 10 Downing Street and spoke to Norma. I had already congratulated John, but this was the first time I had spoken to her since they had moved in from next door.

She sounded the same friendly Norma, unspoilt and down-to-earth as usual, but things were clearly a bit hectic so I kept it short. We exchanged a few words and I began to describe my problem.

I was having a bit of trouble with the telephone, I explained. It was something that had never happened to me before and I didn't know what to do about it. It was driving me mad and I felt hounded and out of my depth. I was under pressure and I didn't want to be an embarrassment to John.

'Don't worry, Terry,' she said. She knew all about that sort of thing and said she'd see what she could do.

For half an hour there was a beautiful silence. Then the telephone rang again and I answered nervously. It could have been my wife, the *Daily Mirror*, the BBC, or 10 Downing Street for all I knew. In fact it was a young lady from British Telecom saying she understood that I had been receiving unwanted telephone calls. Well, I hadn't actually received any because I hadn't been answering it, I told her, perhaps rather pedantically as she became more puzzled. So she gave me my new ex-directory number and bade me farewell.

All was now very quiet, at least for a short while. But, as I was to discover on many occasions, you can't underestimate the perseverance of the ladies and gentlemen of the press. As soon as they found that I had gone ex-directory, they began to appear at the front door again, hammering away as before. They appeared alone now, no longer in packs, but sometimes with a photographer. Instead of trying to ring they would send a dispatch rider, who would stick a note through my letter box asking me to ring them.

25

A nice young man called Shakespeare from the *Evening Standard* was particularly fond of this mode of communication. He may have thought it amused or impressed my neighbours. Mercifully everyone in the street knows that Terry doesn't put on airs and graces or take himself too seriously just because motor cycle messengers are arriving at the door at all hours of the day and night.

Then one day I answered the telephone and it was a reporter. 'How did you get my number?' I asked him. 'I found it on the office computer under news contacts,' he answered.

So much for an ex-directory number.

After this fiery baptism in press relations, I've given up trying to avoid them. I've really become quite used to media people. If I answer their questions I do so truthfully, sometimes at such length and in such detail that I probably bore them. I have heard the odd yawn at the other end of the line. If I don't want to answer because it's something I've been told in confidence, or if it concerns a different newspaper, then I say so. If I feel the question should go to someone else, then again I say so. Sometimes editors have ideas about stories which bear no relation to the facts, the reporters discover. All I ask of reporters is that they should be as straight with me as I am with them. Only very few find such a simple thing impossible. On the whole my dealings with the press have made my life more interesting but I sometimes wonder whether people really understand what a very peculiar situation I find myself in.

As soon as John became Chancellor people began to ask me odd questions about him, but when he became Prime Minister their inquiries became really quite bizarre. Reporters and even friends would ask, for example, whether it was true that he dyed his hair grey. Can you imagine anyone doing that, especially if they are in politics where time is of the essence and where apparently there is a premium on eternal youth? As the owner of a head of hair similar to John's, but slightly greyer, I suppose I am in a better position than anyone else to scotch this canard, but I have never been very successful. What I say to these people is, haven't they heard of hair being bleached in the sun? When I come home from my annual holiday at Butlin's in Bognor, my hair is almost completely white, but it returns to its normal shade a few days later. Well, John travels to far more exotic places than I do. In his job he has to buzz around the world like an astronaut and, unlike me, rarely spends a full week at home. He also has to appear at press conferences where, if my life-long observation of variety shows serves me correctly, the rear lighting is sometimes pretty funny.

On one occasion I had read a newspaper report that John was worn out, depressed and losing weight, and as newspapers were constantly ringing me up about this story, I telephoned him to ask him how he was. The Downing Street switchboard put me straight through.

'Hello, Terry,' said John cheerfully, 'what can I do for you?'

'I just rang to see how you are,' I said.

'How do I sound?' said the Prime Minister.

'A damn sight healthier than me,' was my reply.

I have been walking with John in the woods at Chequers, the Prime Minister's country retreat, when we have talked about confidential family matters which I won't reveal to anyone. It seems there are always officials and politicians just around the corner making it hard to be private. We never discuss politics, though sometimes I can't resist making the odd joke about current news items. I find our time together becomes ever more precious to me as the years go by. Shirley is sometimes a little exasperated, when she says 'Now come on, John, what's that President Bush or Clinton like? We'd really like to know', only to find that he changes the subject to more mundane matters. But we have to remember that he spends his whole life talking politics, and that family time is precious for him too.

I am sorry to say that we don't see his maroon automatic (because of his knee injury) Mini outside our front door as we did when he was a junior minister – how many chauffeurs, speechwriters and detectives can you fit in a Mini? In the old days he and Norma and the children used to come for a pre-Christmas get-together, but now it's all too complicated. He has visited us once in Wallington since he became Prime Minister, arriving at 7.45 one evening after finishing work in Downing Street.

We had asked him for 7 pm, but of course we knew how busy he was. I had laid out a cold buffet in the dining room, just in case he was held up in a meeting, as indeed he was. But 7.45 wasn't bad – as punctual as you can expect from anyone these days. Shirley had ham, turkey, sausage rolls, wedges of pork pie and flan laid out in a fan shape, and various cheeses. I was quite pleased with my handiwork, arranging it on the dishes for Shirley while she cooked, but sorry I forgot the parsley. Not that John would complain about such detail because he's like me and he'll eat anything – but unlike me he manages to keep his youthful figure.

It was like old times, quite a family reunion, with our widowed sister Pat, who lives nearby in Croydon, and her son and daughter who had an 18-month-old son John hadn't seen before. John was in sparkling entertaining form and stayed for three hours, spending most of the evening cuddling the baby and talking about the family.

'It was just my old John,' said Shirley afterwards. There was no sign that he was under any stress. In fact we quite forgot he was Prime Minister.

More often we meet in Downing Street, when I go there to exchange birthday or Christmas presents for members of the family, or perhaps to discuss a problem that's been raised by my friends or the press. If he isn't too busy he usually comes down and has a word, or I go up for a cup of tea in his private apartment. I think it must be the most exclusive spot for a cup of tea in London.

People ask me if it seems odd popping into No 10 for a cup of tea. Why should it? While John is Prime Minister it is both his office and his town flat. What is more natural than visiting one's own brother or sister-in-law when one happens to be in the district? Sometimes John may be too busy, or away, but I may be lucky and catch Norma if she has time between her many engagements. We often have long chats, and sometimes we have lunch together.

On one occasion I have a nasty suspicion I ate the Prime Minister's lunch without him putting in an appearance at all. There was another time, when I had some Christmas presents to deliver, when I really didn't expect to see him because I knew he had arrived back from Washington that morning and was off the Yugoslavia in the afternoon. But when I arrived, there he was, as welcoming as ever, asking if I could stay for lunch. As we sat down – John, Norma and myself – I had to confess that I couldn't manage lunch because I had just bought a pie at Victoria Station, sharing it with the ducks in St James's Park. I had a good chat with them, however, and a very nice cup of tea.

2

Father in America

My younger brother may well have been named after our great-grandfather John Ball, a publican who came from several generations of locksmiths living in the West Midlands in the mid-nineteenth century, but I am not sure about this. Some people, especially members of the press whenever they question our legitimacy or claim there is something pretentious about our background, have suggested that the Prime Minister should be called John Ball, but the fact is that he has always been called John Major, from the moment my father registered him by that name.

Father's original name was Tom Ball but his stage name was Tom Major. By the time he started his garden ornament business in the early 1930s he was known as Tom Major-Ball. Our elder brother Aston, who died at birth, was registered by Father, who signed as Thomas Ball, giving his full name as Abraham Thomas Ball. When my sister Pat was born, my mother signed the register, giving the father's name as Thomas Abraham Major-Ball. Two years later, when I appeared on the scene, it was Father's turn to sign again, this time as A.T. Ball, with Abraham Thomas Ball as his full name. On this occasion it was the registrar who added the Major in the forename column next to Terry because I didn't have a second Christian name. By the time John came along eleven years later the situation had changed again. This time my mother signed the form as Gwendolin Major and giving Thomas Major as the name of the baby's father. So John has been John Major since his birth was registered and, contrary to some suggestions in the press, has never changed his name for political reasons.

What I do know is that by the time of John's christening Father had clearly come to like the no-nonsense sound of John Major and was determined that his baby son should not have a second name. Just as eleven years previously I had been christened simply Terry – I am not even Terence – John would be plain John. He was absolutely furious therefore, my mother told me, when one of the godmothers, a friend of my mother's called Miss Fink, decided without consulting anyone that the baby was going to be called John Roy Major. I well remember Miss Fink as the area supervisor for the Chain Library in Central Road Worcester Park where my mother used to work during the war. She had long, perfectly manicured finger nails and she always smoked Passing Cloud cigarettes. However, for me her claim to fame will not be her finger nails or her cigarettes. She will always be the person who just happened to be holding my baby brother at the font when the vicar asked what the child's name was to be. 'John Roy,' said Miss Fink as Father silently fumed. And John Roy it is, as far as baptism is concerned.

John's namesake, my great-grandfather John Ball, was the fourth of seven children of Joseph Ball, a locksmith born in Willenhall in the West Midlands in 1785. The 1841 census shows the family doing comfortably well, owning a house, a shop and a garden and employing three apprentices and a female servant. Although he was only 21 at the time John, also a locksmith by trade, is listed as the owner of a public house. By the time he was 29, married to Caroline Smith, daughter of a butcher, he owned several houses and a brewhouse. Later in life he was described as a victualler and beer retailer, licensee of the Bridge Tavern in Lane Head (near Walsall), a pub which exists today, and owner of several more houses.

They had six children of whom Grandfather Abraham, born in

1848, was the second. Two of his brothers died as children. A third became a coachbuilder and went with his family to live in Wales.

Abraham married Sarah Anne Marrah, daughter of a miner, and they had a son Tom, Father, born in 1879, and an adopted son Alfred who was born in 1877. The family lived in Bloxwich near Walsall in the West Midlands until the mid-1880s when Abraham, a master bricklayer, set off in search of lucrative employment building blast furnaces for the Andrew Carnegie Steel Works in Pittsburgh, Pennsylvania. Builders were much in demand in this rapidly developing industrial community and Grandfather did well. Later he set up his own building business in Pennsylvania, probably near Philadelphia, and didn't bring his family back to England until Tom was about 17 and Alfred 19. Father therefore spent all his formative years and his schooling in America and had many colourful tales of his childhood to tell us when we were brought up in south London.

He spoke, for example, of sailing on the SS *Indiana* from Liverpool to Philadelphia, telling us that the journey took about three weeks and that some of the poorer migrants from the continent, travelling as deck passengers, were fed with salted herrings from a barrel like sea lions in a zoo. Mercifully, he was able to afford a cabin for his family. When I visited the New York City Library in November 1993 I found a picture of the SS *Indiana*, a storm-tossed primitive early steamship belonging to the American Line with two masts, presumably for stability rather than speed. I could see that Father wasn't exaggerating when he talked about the hardships of the voyage, and I have learned over the years that many of the wilder stories he told about his adventures were actually understatements of the truth. I can imagine that such a journey would make a life-long impression on a child of five or six, and I am thankful that when I made my first crossing of the Atlantic more than 100 years later I was in the first-class cabin of one of Mr Richard Branson's jumbo jets in safety and comfort.

Father used to say that as a child he joined one of the local fife-and-drum bands in Pennsylvania, and that he twice performed as a drum major in front of the then President, Grover Cleveland, who had two separate terms in the White House, 1885-9 and 1893-7. It was probably one of the first occasions when he came to use the name of 'major'. I like to think that President Cleveland saw drum-major Ball in Pittsburgh almost exactly 100 years before President Clinton welcomed his son there as Prime Minister Major.

There is no documentary evidence of all this, but I have no reason to doubt it. Why should there be any papers to prove that his father went as a master builder to America? It is known that Father kept old papers in a trunk, referring to life in America and to his work on the trapeze, but sadly the trunk was lost many years ago when we moved from Worcester Park in Surrey to Brixton. This has never bothered me at all until recently but just before the Prime Minister's visit to Pittsburgh early in 1994 I received several telephone calls from local newspaper reporters, notably from a young lady called Ellen Perlmutter of the *Pittsburgh Post Gazette*. Despite strenuous digging she could find no evidence that Father's family had ever been to Pittsburgh. (It so happens – I had myself discovered in the New York Library – that he just missed the 1880 census and the 1900 one.) As there was nothing to prove that Father had been there, there was a strong suggestion that the whole story had been invented by the White House as a vote-winning exercise in a congressional election year. They ran a headline saying: Why is this man (John Major) coming here?

Well, I was able accidentally to be of some assistance here, telling Ellen Perlmutter that my father used to say that he lived in the foothills of the Allegheny mountains, that he could pick peaches from his bedroom window and that he used to dig the arrowheads from the bark of trees in an old Indian battlefield called Fall Hollow.

'Fall Hollow?' exclaimed Miss Perlmutter. 'Where's that?'

'I don't know,' I said. 'You tell me.'

Miss Perlmutter then got to work and discovered that there had once been a place called Fall Hollow in the suburbs of Pittsburgh but for several generations it had been called by a different name. This seemed sufficient evidence that stories of Tom Ball's childhood in Pittsburgh, improbable though they might sound, had not been invented by the White House, or my father, or for that matter by me. Father used to say that the chairs in our dining-room had been across the Atlantic four times. Why should anyone invent a domestic detail like that?

It was during his time in America that Father first became interested in the circus. He used to say he taught himself gymnastics and acrobatics, practising in the cellar of his father's by now independent building premises. At the age of eight, he said, he was the top man in a four-man pyramid, and as a teenager he was performing on the flying trapeze without a net – to attract a larger crowd and a higher fee.

Father's career on the trapeze is understandably the one that most captivates the media. It is a rich vein of cartoons and one-liners about tight ropes, balancing acts between triumph and disaster, death plunges, that sort of thing. In fact, however, although it was a colourful episode and one which he enjoyed immensely, it was just a brief phase in his life, with no more documentary evidence to support it than any other. Indeed, as no one knows the name he used as a trapeze artist (it was not Tom Ball or Tom Major), it is an impossible subject to research. But somehow the media, who like this story, have never doubted that he really was a trapeze artist and occasionally, of course, a clown. I am grateful to them in a sense, because media interest will perhaps eventually uncover a much-needed fact or two. I well remember that trunk in the bathroom, a large black one with reinforced edges, containing such exotic items as a ginger wig, an evening cane and an opera hat, which as a child I played with, popping it out and collapsing it over and over again. There were also greasepaints, band parts, false whiskers and a black jacket edged in silk. My sister Pat recalls a trapeze costume with a stars-and-stripes design, strongly suggesting that it dates from his time in America, and a photograph of Father wearing this costume.

There were more treasures dotted around the workshops, including a wooden practice baton and several Indian clubs made of papier mâché built onto strong wooden handles and covered with brightly covered foil in intricate patterns. These were used by my parents when they practised in the garden. Often my sister would be practising her acrobatics at the same time and one of them would break off to help her. There was also a wicker basket containing dozens of signed photographs and the folding camera my father used for making large posters for his theatrical performances.

The people who bought our bungalow in Worcester Park, Tom and Yvonne Canter, said they found some strange things in the attic when they put on a new roof in the 1950s. There was the ginger wig I have just mentioned, a white clown's costume and what Yvonne describes as some 'funny feet', large plastic ones presumably for clowning. All these went on a bonfire, but they sent some sheet music to a jumble sale. There were some old books, including a Sunday-school prize belonging to Father, which they later returned to us. I also have a newspaper article in which my father and members of the cast of one of his revues talk about the trapeze and the show to a local reporter.

Some circus experts have suggested to me that Father only did static trapeze, but I am sure they are talking about the later parts of his stage career. He often talked to me about the flying trapeze and it seemed to me as a child a pretty convincing, not to say alarming, account. I should perhaps say that my father never sat us down as children to tell us about his extraordinary life. I rather wish he had, because I might have made a conscious effort to take a note of it. But he was a wonderful story-teller, and always had a stream of anecdotes to entertain or instruct us, whether we were at work or play.

He was of course rather an old parent – 53 when I was born in 1932 and 64 when John arrived in 1943 – so he probably didn't play with us much as other fathers do. Instead he had this wealth of experience with which he would regale us as we sat goggle-eyed on his knee, or on the arm of his chair. He sang us music-hall songs, some of which he had composed himself, and he could tell us the correct grip for the trapeze, wrist to wrist with fingers clasping the other's arms, something which was verified for me when I met some trapeze artists recently in Blackheath. He told me how important clowns were, that everyone in the circus had to be able to play the clown to help the regular clowns, just as everyone had to be available for packing up the circus and setting up camp somewhere else. The circus was a truly democratic environment. I vividly recall him telling me the importance of the catcher in the trapeze. No matter how good the flyer was, my father used to say, if the catcher's timing was out, or if he failed to make a clean catch, it could spell disaster or even death. I believe Father gained considerable experience as a trapeze catcher while he was in America. Unfortunately there is no equivalent of a sound catcher in the world of modern politics.

In an interview with the local priest for a church magazine shortly before his death Father speaks of his interest in acrobatics and gymnastics and of the flying trapeze. The article says his adventures were for a while in this field. He speaks of the travelling booths of such famous pugilists as Gentleman Jim Corbett and John L. Sullivan, where his job was to draw a crowd for the seller of the universal cure-all. Back in England he talks of working in residential circuses or the travelling galas organised by people such as Wilders. He then developed his skills as a character actor and comedian, saying he was near the top of the bill for the opening performance of the Birmingham Hippodrome. He has several songs to his credit and, when working with the Irish comedian Hugh Dempsey, Father managed the act, wrote the songs and did his own turn as an acrobat, all for thirty shillings a week.

All these skills he somehow acquired as a teenager in America while continuing with his normal schooling. Despite this he said he did well at school, and he told the same church magazine that he was offered a Girard scholarship which might have taken him to West Point military academy. Once again there is no firm evidence, but my enquiries have shown that Girard Scholarships were set up some years before by an industrialist in Pittsburgh.

Whether he would have been of the calibre of such distinguished contemporaries as Generals Eisenhower or Macarthur was never put to the test because in the late 1890s Grandfather brought the whole family back to England, almost certainly straight back to the Midlands. There are records of Father playing water polo for Walsall Swimming Club in 1896 and of various swimming proficiency certificates for him and his brother Alfred between 1896 and 1899.

In these three years Father seems to have become a leading light in Walsall Swimming Club, winning individual and club races, and playing water polo against such clubs as Dudley, Birmingham Leander and Smethwick. Perhaps in accordance with his strictures that you should always be prepared to play the clown, he won a canoe race in comic costume in July 1897 dressed as a ballerina and in September a prize for best comic costume winning a two-length swimming race dressed as a 'New Woman' in bloomers. Then at the club's annual dinner in November 1898 Mr T. Ball is on record as providing the last item in the evening's entertainment, an exhibition of American mace-swinging.

Father's stage career began to get under way in the first few years of this century. In 1901 or 1902 he was the star comedian at Frank

Selby's Mermaid show in Liverpool, and afterwards he went on a tour with the leading lady, Kate Edith Grant, who was to become his first wife many years later in 1910.

Long before they married Tom and Kitty were to become a celebrated music-hall double act, usually known as Drum and Major, sometimes Tom and Kitty Major, or occasionally in pantomime as Tom Drum and Miss Kitty Major. Their first recorded engagement, although there were almost certainly earlier appearances, was in August 1902 at the Grand Theatre, Stockton-on-Tees. Towards the end of his music-hall career my father could say he had played in every English town that had a theatre. It is a claim that few people could make today, despite the fact that there are far fewer theatres. This was the age before the advent of the cinema, when the music hall represented all that was best in show business. And Tom and Kitty were at the top of their profession.

For many years they had a regular advertisement on the front page of *The Stage*, except when they went abroad (they toured in Canada, the United States and South America) when it was transferred to the back page. It was a true partnership, with Kitty writing songs and monologues as well as performing them.

There was a mysterious interlude in 1903 and 1904 when they went to South America. Father often used to talk to us about his time in Uruguay and Argentina, and indeed he spoke of it in a magazine article which was published a few days after his death. It appears that they were in Uruguay at a time of extreme political unrest and that Father, who had momentarily lost his passport, was accidentally drafted into one of the Uruguayan armies. Due to language difficulties the name Major was mistaken for an army rank, and Father was given a white armband and put in charge of a small group of men issued with suspect rifles which, according to Father, were a greater danger to them than to the enemy. He said the two sides were known as the Reds (the Liberals or Colorados) and the Whites (the Conservatives or Blancos). I don't know which side Father was on but presumably the whites. He said he marched the men out of the town and then dismissed them. It wasn't a glorious moment in his career, and he never claimed that it was. He brought home a very large knife with an ornate silver handle which for many years was in our workshop in Camberwell. He said it was a gaucho's knife, and he spoke with great respect for the gauchos who he said were completely fearless. He also had a powerful-looking pocket revolver which he brought back from South America. While in Argentina, he once said he was given a job in a gambling den, winning back money for regular clients who had been cheated. The club didn't like to accuse its supposedly respectable members of cheating so they employed Father to take part in a game to find out who was the guilty party. Then he would win the money back from them, subsequently losing it back to the players who had been deprived. The dishonest players would leave the game quietly, with their reputations intact. But it was a risky business, and you will gather that my father, on top of all his other abilities, was skilful with a pack of cards. He often demonstrated spectacular card tricks to us as children, and it has always surprised me that they never seemed to be part of his professional repertoire, but neighbours used to say that he often did card tricks at his sports club and sometimes his local pub.

Many years later Father was once called upon to use the skills he learned in the Argentinian casino when he encountered some cardsharps on a train on their way back from the races. The two tricksters had done very well on the horses and thought they would round off their day by fleecing fellow travellers. They hadn't reckoned on my father who won all their money back off them and distributed it throughout the compartment. Father was also a master of judo but said it was always unwise to demonstrate this, on the grounds that the victor gets the blame when someone is hurt. He had once overwhelmed a boastful fellow who threw a punch at him in a pub and considered himself fortunate that no one was injured when the man fell near a table.

Tom and Kitty married in Bromsgrove in 1910 when Father was 31 and Kitty 36 – she was a widow. At that time they lived on a farm in Catshill near Bromsgrove, but later, with the help of a relative called Florence Spencer but known to us as Aunt Florrie, they built their own house called Drumcote at Higher Heath Prees in Shropshire. Grandfather Abraham (who lived to the age of 83, dying in 1931, his wife having died in 1919) was of course a builder, and no doubt he helped with advice in this ambitious project, but his sight was by now very poor and he could not be relied on. There was a story that when he was an elderly man he once went missing. He was subsequently found up a tree sawing off a branch while sitting on the wrong side of the cut.

Throughout the twenties Drum and Major were frequently reviewed in *The Stage* in places as diverse as Lincoln, Eccles, Bedford and Wolverhampton, albeit in a rather wooden prose style, commenting on their melodious music, attractive scenery and graceful dancing. It was often described as a bright and tuneful show. 'Tom Major is presenting his special edition revue "A Fantasy" in seven scenes here this week with marked success' was said of a performance at the Sandonia Theatre in Stafford on 1 February 1923. 'The revue goes with a swing and there is plenty of fun. Tom and Kitty Major are clever mirth-makers. Their sketch After the Overture is cleverly acted. Bert Brierly (light comedian and dancer) ably assists Tom Major and sings some capital songs.'

After they appeared at the Hippodrome in Bury, *The Encore* said: 'Mr and Mrs Major are the central stars of a galaxy of minor satellites. ... This duo of clever comedians are nothing if not enterprising, either in the quality of their farcical stunts or in their endeavour to present a first-class production.'

'Kitty Major is prominent as a red-haired "slavey" with a penchant for speaking her mind, investing the part with an abundance of funny eccentric comedy' ran *The Stage*'s review of their performance at the Queen's Theatre in Poplar. 'Tom Major scores a success as a policeman of distinctly unusual appearance and attainments.' In Newcastle-under-Lyme Kitty was described as 'a comedienne who puts plenty of life into her work.' In Gainsborough the local paper said she was the only star comedienne who claimed Gainsborough as her native town.

Kitty once wrote a nine-verse patriotic monologue which contained the rousing lines:

> And can you ever remember a Tommy,
> A Swaddie, a Tiffy, or Jack,
> Hear a word said against Mother England,
> And not biff the foreigner back?

Over the years they appeared on the same bill as such well-known music hall names as Marie Lloyd, Lupino Lane, Wal Pink, Joe O'Gorman, Randolph Sutton, Dan Leno Junior, Dolly Harmer, Nellie Wallace, Gertie Gitana, Maskelyne and Devant, Ossi Souplissi, Fred Karno's comedians and Coram and Mills, the mother and father of the Beverley Sisters.

The Drum and Major act continued well into the 1920s, when they were joined by an attractive young speciality dancer named Gwen Coates, daughter of a Gainsborough grocer's assistant. She was about 17, and 26 years younger than my father, when she answered an advertisement for dancers at the time that Father's show visited the area. Gwen and her cousin Daisy had been trained at a local dancing school run by the splendid Miss Girdlestones, but Gwen's father, Harry Coates, was not at all keen for his daughter to become a dancer. Daisy tells me it was Gwen's mother Ada who arranged for her to attend the audition which won her the job. I am very grateful to Ada for this because after Kitty's death Gwen was to become Tom's second wife and of course our mother.

In the early days Kitty was very much a chaperone to Gwen. They worked closely together until her death six years later. Once, much to Father's irritation, Mother and her partner Glad were caught by him moonlighting together in a nearby cinema to make money for new clothes. Father was annoyed because their act was good and their appearance drew customers away from his own theatre. He only noticed when his own box-office takings went down. On one occasion he was particularly furious that Gwen had had her lovely long hair cut off because the bob was in fashion, and he had to re-choreograph her act in a hurry to take account of this. It was probably under Father's tuition that Mother was to become an expert baton and Indian club swinger. This had been his speciality from an early age, but she became almost as good at it as he was. Mother's stage name was Gwen Glen and she had a partner called Gladys Glade, so the pair of them were known as Glade and Glen. I have a photograph of my mother playing in a pantomime as Little Tommy Tucker in 1926 and several others of her in Tarzan's Wooing, wearing some quaintly dated costumes. The *Gravesend and Dartford* reporter commented on this 'acrobatic dance by Glade and Glen' in 1924: 'The dance is entitled Tarzan's Wooing in which two graceful young ladies exhibit much originality and skill. Tom Major who is responsible for training these artistes is to be congratulated.'

I remember Mother as a formidable dancer. She could do the splits as an old lady, even when she was so frail and breathless that she couldn't get up again unaided.

Kitty died in June 1928 after a long illness as a result of an accident with a stage prop. Father married Mother in 1929 after what some might think was an indecently short interval, but the truth is that during her illness Kitty had expressed the wish that if she died Tom and Gwen should marry. The three of them had always been close, and indeed Mother had been looking after Father throughout Kitty's illness. Father kept his second marriage fairly quiet, not even telling his landlady at his digs in Smethwick. On the morning after the wedding she was said to be very shocked, when she took him his breakfast in bed, to find my mother in bed with him and refused to give her any breakfast until she had produced her marriage certificate.

It was in 1930, the year after his second marriage, that Father seems to have decided to give up show business. He was by this time 51, which was too old for some of his acrobatic tricks, and the death of his wife Kitty had been a shock to him and had affected his act. More importantly he was about to start a family: Aston was born prematurely in June 1929 but died at birth, Pat arrived in June 1930 and I was born two years later. Travelling was not conducive to family life. Mother's was a very good stage act, but she never pretended to be a stage partner to Father in the same way that Kitty had been for 27 years, for she was principally a dancer. A stage partnership is like a marriage. Once a double act has finished it is very difficult to make another one, however talented the individuals may be, as many a showbusiness character has discovered. There was also the encroachment of cinema on music-hall entertainment. Perhaps Father was one of the first to see the writing on the wall.

It was some time in the early 1930s that Father stopped describing himself as an actor. He appears on Pat's birth certificate in 1930 as an 'actor', while on mine in 1932 he is a 'fuel agent'. He was, I believe, selling bulk supplies of coal and coke at the time, but this was one of several different things he experimented with to make ends meet.

It was at about this time that he first started making garden ornaments in a room (which later became my bedroom) in the bungalow in Worcester Park. His first moulds, I'm told, were hollow celluloid ducks bought at Woolworths. He filled them with cement and held the moulds together with rubber bands. Then he painted them with lacquer paint and set off to sell them with a delivery bicycle with a large basket on the front. With his experience of showbiz he was a very effective salesman, and Major's Garden Ornaments, as it was called, began to flourish.

As it expanded and he needed to produce ornaments in large numbers, he taught himself the difficult art of making plaster moulds, and he also bought a van so that he could deliver throughout southern England. Soon he began to take on staff and paid them top wages. The business expanded and he started to supply sand and cement, ballast and turf, and he offered a landscaping service.

During the 1930s when the country was supposed to be in the grip of a depression Major's Garden Ornaments went from strength to strength. Father had flourishing outlets all over southern England and the future was looking rosy. Then the war came and his loyal employees began to be called up for military service. Worse still, garden ornaments were the last thing people needed during the war. So he closed down the firm and went into Civil Defence, and Mother took a job in a library. By the end of the war, he was in his late sixties and in failing health, but with a young family. Even for a man with as many different skills as Father it was going to be very difficult to pick up the pieces again.

3

War Breaks Out

I was seven at the outbreak of war, and I can clearly remember Neville Chamberlain's announcement on the wireless. Although we all knew from our history lessons that it would mean a lot of fighting, I don't think any of us children understood what it meant in terms of food rationing and shortages and loved ones being far from home. In Worcester Park we were lucky to be on the periphery of the air raids. Although we had our fair share of bombs and rockets, these were often dropped by the raiders on their way home. They often seemed to save one or two bombs for the local sewage works near the rear of the bungalow, and the big mobile gun on the railway also seemed to be a prime target. Nor was it too healthy being as close to Kenley and Croydon airports as we were.

On the day we saw the first enemy aircraft over Worcester Park I was playing with my sister Pat in the garden. I was seated on the lawn on a big blue cloth which had once been used to cover a bookmaker's stand. I believe Father had obtained it when a bookmaker had disappeared without waiting to pay out his winners, a not uncommon occurrence with on-course bookies in those days. We also possessed a large two-leaved blackboard which opened like a book, very handy for children but taller than both of us, which had come Father's way for the same reason. On reflection, Father was obviously a racing fan in what little time his business left him.

When the aircraft swooped low over the garden I rose to my feet. It was so close that I could see the swastikas on its wings but I wasn't aware, at this stage, that this meant it was a German aircraft. Mother was in no doubt, however, and ran out into the garden in a rare state of panic almost before the sirens had sounded, scooping up the bookmaker's cloth with our toys and hustling us indoors. It was the first air raid of the war and I wondered what was to come. Later, as things settled down, like most of the children in Worcester Park I became a little indifferent to the war. It was over four years before the next big scare, when a flying bomb landed near the bungalow, spraying broken glass over baby John's cot when he was fifteen months old. This incident prompted our parents to evacuate the family to Norfolk.

The start of the war saw yet another transformation of Father and his fortunes. He was now an air raid warden wearing a white helmet, with a local command centre based in a concrete bunker on the corner of the children's public playground at the top of Longfellow Road. He was much too old to join the army and would never have been accepted anyway, even at the time of the First World War, because of his heart condition. But he took to Civil Defence in good spirit and was soon promoted to become a senior warden, or post-warden, as they were called. Hence the white helmet with 'Warden' written in black lettering, while ordinary wardens had black helmets with white lettering.

The command centre itself was a small solidly constructed brick hut, with a reinforced concrete roof, a strong steel door with a heavy concrete lintel, and a hole at the back covered with a large cast-iron plate fixed with bolts which could be undone to provide an emergency escape route. It was to become a much-loved permanent fixture for children's games in the playground long after the war had ended, and for my father it was quite a reassuring base.

We were lucky that our bungalow was solidly built, so we were allowed to have an Anderson shelter inside the house. Most people had theirs in the garden half-buried in the ground, where of course it could be very cold and damp. Anderson shelters were made of curved corrugated sections fitted together according to the size of the family, and ours could take a single bed and two kitchen chairs.

This was a great improvement on the Morrison shelter, like a table with a heavy angled iron frame, a solid-steel top and wire-mesh sides, which most people had in their houses. You had to crawl into these and you couldn't stand up.

Usually when the raids were bad our bed contained myself, my sister Pat and a girl called Noreen, aged about 5, from next door. Mother and our next-door neighbour Mrs Cowley sat on the two chairs. Her husband was usually out fire-watching and Father was on duty with the wardens, or standing with the neighbours outside the house watching what was going on.

We lay there in the shelter counting the bombs as they dropped, or calculating how far away they were by measuring the seconds from the whistle of the falling bomb to the sound of the explosion. Gradually the adults became quite blasé and stood in the garden watching the guns and the searchlights until the last minute before diving into the shelter. If the local guns weren't firing I was allowed to watch the searchlights swinging round to catch the aircraft in their beams. People would cheer them on, it was like a sport. There was an atmosphere of great excitement. Each plane downed was one less to bomb us the next night but, as an adult looking back on it, I am saddened to think that each German pilot was someone's father, son or husband. It's true there are no winners in war: we are all victims in some way.

My biggest hardship was a shortage of sweets. We began to look around for alternatives, in my case one of them was carrots. The lady in the greengrocer's half way up Worcester Park hill used to provide large, juicy, crunchy ones very cheaply and washed them ready for eating. These were much more popular with teachers and parents than liquorice wood, which tended to gather fluff when kept half-chewed in the pocket. My alternative was Ovaltine Tablets from the chemist's shop.

Possibly the worst effect of the war from the family's point of view was the closure of the garden ornament business, which caused a big drop in income. Pat and I had both gone to a private school called Kingsley High School, where the principal gloried in the name of Miss Trott, and to a dancing school called Morgan Juveniles where we were both supposed to be learning to tap-dance, Pat more successfully than me. Now we would have to be taken away and sent to the council school, called Cheam Common School, where Pat started in November 1939 and I followed in April 1940. It must have been a bitter blow for Father who always took the education of his children seriously.

I have few memories of Kingsley, but I'm told I made myself less than popular with the staff by comforting naughty little girls who had been reprimanded by the teacher. My worst memory of the new school was of a chocolate sponge-pudding, which put me off anything resembling a chocolate cake for many years. When the teacher asked 'Anyone for seconds?' I put up my hand before I had even tried my first helping and landed myself with another large bowl of dark brown stodge, which made me feel quite sick. In those days no food was wasted. If you asked for something you ate it, and my struggle with the pudding was only ended by the bell. It wasn't until I was about 35 that my wife Shirley persuaded me that chocolate puddings were a good idea. I also remember being escorted to the head's office, led up some stairs by the ear, for an offence I've long forgotten. Teachers there say such treatment would not be allowed today, but I'm sure it did me no harm. Nor did Cheam Common School do my brother John any harm when he went there for four years, starting in 1950.

John went from Cheam Common to Rutlish Grammar, while Pat went to Nonsuch High School for Girls. I was the only one who failed my 11-plus and went to a secondary modern, Stoneleigh East Central. I have no regrets about this, because it turned out to be a good school with an excellent headmaster, Mr Corner.

My brother John's arrival on the scene in March 1943 was a surprise to me and, I always thought, to everyone else. It was only recently that I discovered this wasn't the case. Fifty years ago mothers might have discussed such matters with girls of Pat's age, but they tended not to mention them to boys of my age. The confusion may have arisen because Father didn't know of the coming birth until some time after the conception whereas my mother did, because she had secretly planned it.

It was a sunny day on 28 March and Pat recalls that she was sitting on the back step preparing vegetables while Mother was inside cooking. She remembers thinking it strange that Mother was wearing a fur coat when it was warm enough to be sitting outside. Then quite suddenly Mother collapsed, the doctor was summoned and she was soon on her way by ambulance to Surrey County Hospital in St Helier where she was admitted with double pneumonia and pleurisy, a serious condition for a pregnant woman of 38.

The next day John was born, a healthy baby at first, but he soon succumbed to a germ which, the hospital later admitted when they cancelled the bill, was introduced into the ward by the nursing staff. Quite soon there was concern for both mother and child, and there is no doubt in my mind that they owed their survival to the dedicated round-the-clock care which the hospital provided. When I first saw John at home some weeks later, I was quite shocked by the weals on his ankles. It looked as if he had been

51

beaten with a thin cane, but Mother explained that these were caused by his many blood transfusions.

Our parents were both very grateful to the hospital for its devoted attention and never bore any ill-will for the fact that John's troubles might have been inflicted by them. Mother later kept in touch with the nurses, on at least one occasion sending them a picture of her healthy baby to reassure them that all was well. Quite recently the sister of one of these nurses sent John a photograph of himself as a baby sitting in a cane chair, a picture of good health, with details of his weight and how he was doing. Mother had sent it to her sister.

Mother made a remarkable recovery, although it was a lasting shock to me to discover that she was as vulnerable to illness as everyone else, and was soon back at work in the Chain Library in Worcester Park, where she was now manageress and librarian. In the first twelve months of his life John must have spent about eight hours a day in that library in his pram which was parked on the floor of the shop, where everyone could see and talk to him and, when he was asleep, in a staff room. I have often thought that this may explain why he has always been a more bookish character than I am. I used to call in at the library most days on my way back from school.

Surprising though it is to some people, I was never in the least jealous of John. Possibly because he was so much younger, I was terribly proud of him, as I always have been. I was old enough to be responsible for pushing him in his pram in Longfellow Road and, having until then been the youngest, I was pleased to have someone I could myself look after. I went to secondary school shortly after he was born, was working when he was five and by the time he was eight was in the army. This meant that although I was nearly as close to him as I was to Pat the relationship was different.

John was born into family circumstances that were very different from Pat's and mine in the early thirties. When we were small children the garden ornament business was just taking off. By the time we were at school it was very successful and the family was comfortably off. Father had two works premises and employed a gardener, who provided cut flowers for the house and tended the fruit trees. We had a sort of nanny. She was officially employed to work for my father's business, but as Mother preferred making ornaments to doing housework they would swap places.

We also had the loving care of Mrs Swain, a neighbour who took us in next door whenever my mother was ill. Mother would always consult her about our health – she was something of an amateur doctor and had strong views on diet. It may be an indication of how well-off we were, or how spoiled as children, that Mother would give us whatever we wanted to eat to ensure a quiet life. She would open some tinned peaches for Pat and some pears for me and we both ate cakes. Mrs Swain, on the other hand, would make us eat plenty of bread-and-butter before we had our cakes.

When John was a child these things weren't just luxuries, they were rarities. Life had become a struggle because of the war. In a curious way John had more freedom than we did because our parents were both too busy to worry about him. For instance when he came home from school he would often go next door to watch Mr Swain doing his garden and Mr Swain would help him with his homework. John also spent a lot of time with the Cowleys, who had a son of his age. Once when Mother was out collecting payments for garden ornaments John and his small friends decided to take in a load of sand which had just been delivered. John's head was gashed with a shovel and it was Mrs Cowley who took him to hospital. That's the way our community worked in those days.

Another local friend, Mrs Brand, told me of a terrifying occasion when her son John was driving his pedal car along the pavement of Green Lane where they lived, with our John riding on the bumper. They rounded some bushes into the road cutting across the path of a startled motorist who braked and swerved, hitting the kerb while the two Johns disappeared down the bank into a brook. He certainly had more freedom than his elder siblings ever had and it probably did him a lot of good in the long run.

I remember the war years as happy ones. We could walk to school in safety. We respected adults and they treated us with respect, although occasionally we went to elaborate lengths to break the rules they invented for us. There was a stream running down the far side of Green Lane that I was forbidden to play in. Naturally this made it an even more attractive proposition to try jumping it. Whenever I got wet Pat would take me home and push me into the goldfish pond in the garden. This ploy convinced Mother the first time. But the second and third time? I think she realised what had happened but let us get away with it.

My nearest brush with death during the war came when a friend of Father's called Uncle Mac, a six-foot-six military policeman who used to track down army deserters and soldiers who had extended their leave, visited our house. Uncle Mac obviously considered himself relaxed and off-duty in my father's company because he left his revolver on my parents' bed, an obvious invitation to young children who like playing cowboys and Indians, as Pat and I did. In one of the most dramatic scenes ever seen in the bungalow Uncle Mac and Father appeared in the bedroom doorway just as Pat pointed the gun at my head saying 'Hands up' in her best cowgirl voice. Uncle Mac said the gun was loaded but we were lucky the safety catch was on, although I find it hard to believe he would have left it unattended if it had been loaded. This story has been elaborated in the press to suggest the that Prime Minister's young life was somehow at risk, so I would like to point out that it would have been a lesser tragedy. It was only me.

John was eventually more streetwise than either of us. After the war while I was in the army John, who owned a female rabbit, established a joint venture breeding rabbits with his friend John

Brand, who owned a male. Father built a hutch and they sold them for sixpence each. Later they went into breeding mice and John, without consulting Mother, would offer a piece of her cake as a bonus for buying three mice. Pat and I would never have got away with this when we had our mouse farm.

All this was in the future, however, and I mention it now only to show how his upbringing differed from Pat's and mine. In our early days Mother was nearly always at home and probably spoiled us terribly. In John's time she had her career and he had to look after himself to a greater extent. She was a wonderful mother, but she was also to become a formidable business lady with a certain toughness and an ability to get on with everyone acquired during her theatrical career, combined with her natural cheek.

The headmaster of my Secondary Modern, Mr Corner, always wore a brown warehouse coat and a beret and usually carried a cane. Although he sounds a comic figure he was a very clever man who loved teaching and I had an instant feeling of respect for him, not just because of the cane, which in fact he rarely used, but because he would have long erudite conversations with my father about his world travels. He knew how much I loved my father and craved his approval, and he knew this would win my attention – to fall out with my father was worse than any school punishment. But Mr Corner also seemed to have travelled as much as my father, which to me was in itself a matter to wonder at.

He got the best out of his pupils with discipline, understanding, humour and basic teaching skills. I remember him in the playground staring intently at the sky until a group of young faces gathered around him looking upwards. 'What are you looking at, sir?' they screamed.

'Nothing,' he replied. 'I'm just trying to teach you to do things for a good reason and not just blindly follow the example of others.'

I gather that he tested the individuality of several generations of pupils in this way. Too many teachers, I have always thought, take the easy option and try to make their pupils behave like sheep. Mr Corner actively encouraged us to be ourselves.

One of the most annoying things about the war was having to carry a gas mask everywhere. We had shelter practices and gas drills every day at school to see how quickly we could put them on. There was a horrible smell of rubber and it was quite difficult to breathe through the filters. Sometimes we would have to wear them during lessons in the shelters. I understand that this was so that we would get used to them, but at the time there was a strong suspicion that it was just a way of keeping little boys quiet.

All this came to an end, after I had been at this school for only ten months, when a flying bomb or doodlebug landed near our house showering John's cot with splinters of glass, as we have seen. I remember the doodlebugs well. Their engines would cut out and there followed a dreadful bang. Mother had just removed John, who was about a year old, from his cot under the bedroom window and was halfway down the hall passage when there was a terrific explosion from the direction of Caldbeck Avenue. When she went back into the room the cot was filled with glass, and it was enough to persuade our parents that time had come to evacuate, and arrangements were made to go to Norfolk.

4

Evacuated

I was in hospital with scarlet fever when the family was evacuated, and as I was allowed no visitors I didn't hear about it until after they had gone. Father brought the news when he came to collect me. I had been taken in a green ambulance to an isolation unit in Banstead, where I lay for several weeks on a mattress under a bed with a sheet of corrugated iron on top for protection. One morning I awoke to find I couldn't move at all and lay there for ages staring at the wall, unable to look round and afraid to call out. Eventually a nurse noticed my tear-stained face and went off to find some cotton wool, bandages and wintergreen lotion. Soon the nurses rubbed me all over with this green liquid and trussed me up like a turkey. It made me feel me feel very hot, as if I was indeed cooking, but it did ease the pain. Even when I was released from Banstead I wasn't allowed to see other children and had to spend a further two weeks on a farm some distance from the rest of the family.

By the time I was reunited with Mother, Pat and John I already quite fancied myself as a countryman. When I first arrived on the farm, as a 12-year-old who had spent his entire life in London, I was astonished to find there were no water taps in the kitchen. The first time I was told to fetch the drinking water from the well I was very embarrassed that I didn't know the galvanised bucket was for fresh water, the enamel one for slops. A friendly farmer's wife put me right about these vital matters, and she provided me with such an abundance of milk and eggs, which were in short supply in town, that I began to think the war was over.

My family were staying in a cottage in a village, where my main recollection is of American GIs, some of whom would get very drunk after an evening in the pub, and of the Jeeploads of military police who arrived to move them on. Soon afterwards we all moved to more peaceful surroundings in a large house containing several evacuee families. There were two large fields and, out of bounds, a large orchard with pigs, stables with horses, and a private garden with tennis courts. Needless to say, it was in the out of bounds parts that we preferred to spend our time. With a new friend called Billy, who came from Romford, I used to explore the haylofts.

We also made friends with some prisoners of war who were responsible for cutting the hedges. They were mostly elderly German soldiers of the pre-war army guarded in a haphazard way by a few English soldiers with guns but no bullets. The Germans would say 'Good morning' or 'Nice day' to us. One day there was a knock on our door and a German sergeant asked if he could borrow some tea as they had left theirs at the camp. Though tea was rationed, Mother didn't like to see anyone, not even a German prisoner of war, go without a cup of tea, so she gave him one of her precious packets. Next day they were back with not only a replacement packet of tea but several sacks of firewood they had chopped for her.

We got on well with these Germans. They said they were sick of Hitler and the Nazis and the war they expected to lose. They were professional soldiers but were glad to be out of the fighting. It seemed so absurd that there we all were, far from home, because of a conflict that none of us wanted. A few days later we saw why we were at war when these civilised gentlemen were replaced by a group of arrogant young thugs with trouble written all over their faces.

They used to shout obscenities at us, and the final straw came when Mother caught a few of them outside the back door trying to teach baby John the Nazi salute. Mother flew at them, and some English and German NCOs came running to see what the commotion was about. They couldn't apologise enough. They reported the matter and said it would never happen again. In fact we didn't see any more prisoners. The next time I encountered Germans was seven years later when I went to Germany on National Service. Once again I found perfectly normal people who didn't want to talk about the war any more than I did.

John made a big impression on an American soldier who had a son of the same age whom he hadn't yet seen. He and another GI made an equally big impression on Pat and me by giving us sweets over the estate boundary fence. We knew of course that we weren't supposed to accept gifts from strange men but my parents had vetted these two and judged them to be OK. Father had by now undergone another of his professional transitions and was working on an American aerodrome. He was thus able to check up on these men. Perhaps as a result of his childhood he was well disposed to all things American, as indeed we all were when we discovered that the base was throwing out near-perfect crates of oranges as pig food. British people rarely saw oranges in those days. The pig farmer would tell us when the next load of oranges was coming, so that we could rummage through the reject crates filling up bags for our family and friends.

I went to the village school in Saham Toney, but Pat, who was at a Grammar School, had to ride a bicycle to the station to catch a train to Thetford. My main accomplishment was to make a replica of a six-gun out of wood, although it turned out more like a revolver. I have memories of picking walnuts in the autumn and having snowball fights in the winter, both of them new experiences for me. I got into trouble for thumping a choir boy in church after he kept flicking me with a rubber band during choir practice (although why I was ever in the choir was a mystery, because I was never a singer like my parents – my singing makes brave men weep) and for chopping down a small tree with an axe the vicar had given me as a strangely inappropriate present at his Christmas party.

I had a very happy time in the country and was sorry when we left Norfolk in April 1945. Just as our lorry was leaving for London a local boy brought my sister a present of a tiny ginger kitten. Later called Saham after our village, he was to become the father of many Worcester Park cats.

Back at Stoneleigh East School I was again under the attentive tutelage of Mr Corner. The poor man despaired a little about my ambition when I was chosen as the star of the school play, to appear as St Augustine, and I asked instead to be the lighting engineer. The drama teacher refused my request and I ended up without a role at all. I have always thought of myself as a practical person rather than a star and have never had any illusions about this. The lighting is what I always wanted to do and I went on to build two or three simple model theatres to light by battery power.

Mr Corner was even more upset when the time came for me to leave school at 15. He and Father wanted me go to technical college, but I was determined to go into the family's garden ornament business and get it going again. To me it was a matter of pride, but to them it was just obstinacy. They arranged interviews at the Labour Exchange, but of course I refused the jobs that were offered. Father was now 68 and getting a little old for garden ornament making. He thought there were better ways for me to earn my living, but reluctantly he agreed to allow me to join the firm.

By this time he had diversified and was making fancy decorative tiles and floral baskets which he sold to Bentalls department store in Kingston, among other outlets. He made wall plaques painted in Chinese lacquer, including a rendering of an Indian chief in full head-dress, one of which was reported recently as still existing in

Australia. He also took delivery of large quantities of cement (by the ton) and sand (usually six cubic yards), as this was the cheapest way to buy. One day a large lorry and trailer, loaded with breeze blocks, arrived and Father said he had exchanged them for a consignment of garden ornaments. This deal was not as mad as it sounds. A man who made breeze blocks had given up this field of expertise to join a partnership leasing a London bomb site to use as a trading and display ground. Father realised that having his ornaments on display in central London could lead to repeat orders. Meanwhile, I was given the job of extending the garage and building a coal bunker with the breeze blocks. We later built a wall which still exists in the front garden of the bungalow.

Father's new hobby was breeding goldfish. He had two ponds for the goldfish and we used to catch them in saucers and put them in a glass tank to grow. I well remember the water butt collecting the rainwater from the roof. He used it for breeding fish food, but for us it was handy for standing on while talking to the Cowleys or for taking a short cut over the fence. Beyond that was the old green shed where Father used to work before the war. Now completely overgrown by a huge rambler rose and very dark although connected by an electric lead to the sitting room, it was a depressing sight with broken Indian clubs still sparkling with gleaming foil and wooden practice batons. At the back of the bungalow was a strip of concrete which Pat and her boyfriend Peter (later her husband) used for ballroom-dancing practice. Pat had a gold medal and bar while he had a silver, so they took this very seriously.

Father was very annoyed to find when he came back from the war that someone had been picking up the ornaments which he had rejected as being less than perfect and was selling them off as antiques. I was therefore given the task of digging a large pit behind the big apple tree at the bottom of the garden to dispose of broken ornaments. He had once sold a load of chipped concrete animals as hardcore for building, and it was these that had turned up

61

covered with moss after being left under trees in an orchard. They were now being distributed for sale at prices greater than Father had charged for the perfect originals.

After the war Father looked into the possibility of vinyl moulds for making garden gnomes, but he found they were too expensive considering the capital we had available.

Now that we no longer had a gardener Father lost interest in growing flowers and went in for vegetables on a large scale. One year we were knee-deep in shallots and poor Mother had to pickle them in 7lb earthenware jars. Next year he grew rows of tomatoes, which never quite ripened, so they had to be made into chutney. There was also a large tree which produced pears which were normally as hard as bullets. Mother found that by preserving the pears in Kilner jars she could transform them into soft and juicy fruit with a nice flavour, but this too was a lot of work for her.

Although Father was as enthusiastic as ever about his various projects he was in a way losing his grip. Increasingly it was Mother who was going out and getting the orders and collecting the debts. Pat left school and did a course in art and dress design at Wimbledon Art College. She also helped out with modelling and painting.

I don't remember John very clearly from this period but I know that from an early age, unlike me, he was very keen on cricket. Pat says she taught him the rules, coaching him with the aid of a library book, which had diagrams showing where to put your fingers on the seam of the ball and on the handle of the bat. The pitch stretched across the street, which was quite safe in those days. There was an alley opposite the bungalow which was used for the bowler's approach in one direction while the garden path was the run-up in the other. A stone pillar I had put up for a gate-post formed the wicket. If the players were chased away they usually resumed the game by the three garages further up the street.

John was in the scouts and seemed quite good at finding bob-a-job tasks. With his friend John Brand he used to shovel hardcore for a neighbour for ten shillings, which wasn't bad money for those days. John Brand says this was the largest sum on their cards at the end of the week. Our John was never short of pocket money and he also kept an eye open for bargains. When a new milk bar opened in the main street John was one of the first to hear that they were giving away free ice creams, dashing around to collect his friend John to go for a free treat. Toni's Milk Bar was later to become the focus of my own social life when I returned from National Service, and it was here that I met my friend Ted Hunt.

1. Tom Major (left) in his Vaudeville days. In the first three decades of this century he performed in
every town in Britain which had a theatre, and in North and South America.

2. *Top:* Bound for Pennsylvania. The SS *Indiana,* in which Tom sailed as a child with his family to America in the 1880s. *Left:* Tom's mother, Sarah Anne Marrah (wife of Abraham Ball), original owner of the distinctive Major upper lip. *Right:* Tom as a young man.

3. *Top:* Drum and Major. Tom Major with his first wife Kitty Grant in the 1920s when they became a celebrated double act. *Left:* Tom and Kitty in more conventional dress. *Right:* Tom made up as a tramp, a photograph which the Prime Minister has commissioned as a painting.

4. Glade and Glen. Tom Major's second wife Gwen Coates (on the left in each of these pictures) in stage costume as a dancer aged about 18. Her partner Gladys (known as Glade) did the lifting while Gwen (Glen) got thrown about.

5. *Above, right & below left:* Tarzan's Wooing, a regular routine by Glade and Glen, with Gladys as Tarzan and Gwen doing the splits, something she was able to do even as an old lady. *Below right:* Gwen in pantomime costume.

6. *Top left:* Tom Major as a country gent in Shropshire in the 1920s where he owned a farm. Later, with the help of his first wife Kitty and cousin Florence Spencer, he built his own house. *Top right:* Garden gnome manufacturer in the 1930s. *Above:* With second wife Gwen in the 1950s.

OUTSIDE MY OLD ROOM
IN DENIMS.

1951

7. *Above left:* Terry with his father at the outbreak of war when Tom gave up the garden ornament business to become an air raid warden.
Above right: Terry in the 30th Field Ambulance at Bad Lippspringe, formerly a sanatorium, then an SS camp, in 1951. *Right:* John in happy days at Worcester Park before financial crisis loomed.

8. *Top left:* A busman's holiday. Terry in Eastbourne on a London Transport day out with his father-in-law who worked on the buses. *Top right:* Shirley just before her wedding. *Above:* After the wedding at Brixton Register Office, left to right, Mrs Dessoy, Barbara Barnes, Aunt Florrie (a cousin), Dick (a friend of John's), Leonie Hunt (Ted's wife), Milly (Shirley's mother), Peter Dessoy (Pat's husband), Shirley, John, Terry and Mother.

9. *Top left:* Terry and Shirley cut the cake. *Top right:* Shirley with Terry's best man Ted Hunt. Ted's black Ford had livened up Terry's bachelor days. *Left and below:* Shirley and Terry visit Sheerness during their honeymoon, when they stayed in Aunt Rose's chalet on Sheppey.

10. Some Major dogs. *Above left:* Pat with Butch in Worcester Park – the breeze block wall was built by Terry. *Above right:* John with Butch, now much older, in Burton Road – with the Christmas tree he and Terry found dumped in Brixton Market.
Below left: Butch with a gnome and a Peter Pan figure. *Below right:* Butch's replacement, Whiskey.

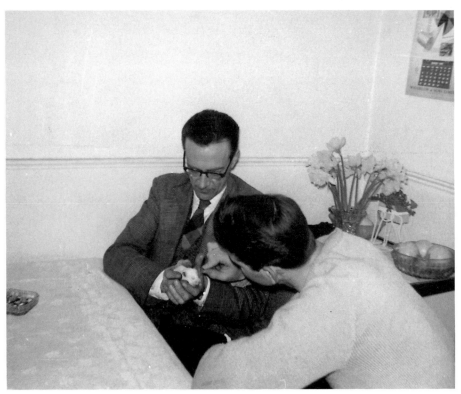

11. *Top left:* Gnomes from home. John surveys the handiwork of Major's Garden Ornaments in Burton Road – right, an apple gnome, left, a woodcutter gnome, with a birdbath, an ivy tub and three sitting babes on rocks. *Top right:* Grandmother Milly with Fiona at home in Thornton Heath. *Above:* John feeding pills to hamster Christine (held by brother-in-law Peter) in a sadly unsuccessful all-night vigil.

12. John and Norma's wedding, photographed by Terry. *Top:* The reception was at Brixton Town Hall, where Clive Jones made the speech as best man. *Above:* On the steps of St Matthew's Church, left to right, Norma's mother Dee Johnson, John, Norma, Clive Jones, Norma's cousin Claire. Front row, John's nieces Fiona and Mandy.

13. John Major as Chairman of the Housing Committee at Lambeth Council, seen here in 1971 with Julian Amery (second from right), then Minister for Housing. At Lambeth John Major won the respect even of left wingers such as Ken Livingstone. John has always known where he is going, says Terry, and it is no surprise that he has got to the top.

14. *Above:* A squirrel photographed by Terry at Hotham Park, near Bognor, and *left:* Terry relaxing in County Suite – just two of the attractions of Butlins. *Below:* Shirley, her leg in plaster, at home with Mark, just before the Butlins holiday in which Terry suffered from a bad back.

15. *Above:* The Aquasplash at Butlins, near Bognor. Terry was at first sceptical of the charms of Butlins, thinking it would be too much like his army camp, but when he found en suite showers and modern facilities he became an enthusiast. *Right:* With Fiona at Butlins.

16. Worcester Park and Brixton. *Top:* Tom and Gwen's bungalow in Longfellow Road where they started the garden ornament business and brought up their three children. The front garden wall is made from concrete blocks moulded by Tom and Terry and the garage had a side entrance so that the neighbours could use it for their new car. *Above:* Coldharbour Lane where the family occupied two rooms on the top floor.

17. Brixton and Wallington. *Top:* The house in Burton Road near Myatt's Fields where John spent his teenage years and joined the Young Conservatives. The home of Tom and Gwen, Terry, Pat (and later her husband Peter), John, a dog, a hamster, a budgerigar and a jackdaw. *Above:* Terry's and Shirley's house near Croydon which was besieged by reporters when John became PM.

18. *Top:* Terry and Shirley with the Beverley Sisters (whose parents performed with Tom and Kitty Major), Joy at the back and twins Babs and Teddy in their dressing room at the Secombe Centre in Sutton. 'I've never seen a man look so smug,' said John when he saw this picture. *Above:* Terry with trainees at Zippo's Circus.

19. Zippo's Circus. *Top:* Terry presents a certificate to a trainee clown. *Above left:* With David Drummond and a Tom and Kitty Major poster. *Above right:* Terry and Zippo discuss the trapeze grip once used by Tom Major.

20. *Top:* Central Park, New York, November 1993. On his first trip overseas Terry says he could happily have stayed for a fortnight. *Above:* Virgin flyer. Richard Branson's young ladies were charming and one of them reminds Terry of his mother.

21. *Top:* Seeing Manhattan by helicopter. Terry and James ready to fly around the Statue of Liberty and the World Trade Center. 'I felt like a bird,' says Terry. *Above:* Near Times Square. Terry finds New Yorkers, even cops and cab drivers, always ready to stop for a chat.

22. Terry and Shirley outside their house in Wallington, Surrey.

23. *Top:* American roots: John Major with Bill Clinton in Pittsburgh in February 1994. Local newspapers could find no hard evidence of Tom Major's childhood in Pennsylvania until Terry provided vital clues. *Above:* Pat and Terry.

24. *Top:* South London home-owner: Wallington people are proud of their homes, says Terry, and fond of their leafy surroundings. *Above:* John goes to his elder brother's house for a family gathering in January 1994. Time was too precious to discuss politics.

5

Moving to Rented Rooms

After the war we were still a happy family, but compared with the atmosphere of optimism when Father first set up the garden ornament business in the early 1930s a touch of the enthusiasm had now gone. Father was becoming increasingly depressed by the Attlee Labour Government and was beginning to make plans to emigrate with the family to Canada, a country he knew well. I daresay he was thinking that his own happy childhood in America was a model for us all and would have gone to the United States if he had the chance, but Canada House was taking immigrants, so that is where he went.

Father had always been a true-blue Tory. His mother had a set of china for special occasions, such as when the Tory MP came to tea, as he did from time to time. Father would often get involved in heated political discussions. On one occasion in 1948 I was working late in the garage moving things about when there was a terrible noise on the pavement outside the bungalow. I put my ear to the door and heard Father in full spate with a much younger man from up the road who was saying, 'Tory bastard, you need your head punching.' Even at the age of 16 I was all ready, with sleeves rolled up, to go to the rescue, but while I was sneaking around the side of the house Mother caught me. She warned me forcefully to keep out of the arguments of adults. 'Your father is more than capable of dealing with that man,' said Mother, whose political views were very similar to her husband's.

Father blamed Attlee for everything. He could see very little prospect of getting back to the good life he had enjoyed before the war, at least while the Socialists were in power. Even if the Conservatives were returned at the next election it would take them too long to get the country out of the mess it was in now, so he decided to sell the house and the business and go to Canada. It was a desperate move, which would have completely altered the course of our lives but, the way Father saw it, this was what was needed. He was too old to qualify for an assisted passage, but he thought he could just about afford it.

After thirty years in show business he had learned to take people at their word, doing deals with a shake of the hand. It was this that led to his downfall when an apparently wealthy widow and her sister offered to buy Major's Garden Ornaments. The widow had a gentleman friend who needed to be kept in gainful employment, and part of the deal that my father agreed was that I would teach this man the garden ornament business from top to bottom, from models to mould-making, from crocodiles to flamingoes, in the transitional period.

From my own point of view this wasn't a productive time. My father was paying the widow's friend and myself a wage out of the money he was supposed to receive for the business, while neither of us was turning out as many garden ornaments as I had previously done on my own. The poor man simply hadn't grasped in full measure what his love for this widow entailed. As far as garden ornaments were concerned, his heart wasn't in it. I wouldn't like to say that making garden ornaments dealt a death blow to their relationship, but I do know that the widow and her boyfriend quarrelled and parted long before I was able to bring him up to the standards of excellence that I would have wished for Major's Garden Ornaments.

Needless to say the two ladies weren't interested in learning these skills for themselves, and when this man went out of their lives, so, just as dramatically, did their interest in making garden ornaments. They said they were going to pull out and they wanted their money back, but Father pointed out that most of this money had by now been spent – on putting the firm back on a debt-free footing, on new moulds, equipment and premises, and on paying wages to me and her much-missed gentleman friend.

Father tried to impress on the two ladies that they owned the business and that, if they wished to find someone else to run it for them, his son Terry would once again oblige. They replied with devastating candour that garden ornaments were not their cup of tea, that it might as well have been a sausage factory for all they cared, that they only wanted it to keep their friend happy – a goal which sadly the business had failed to achieve. They accused Father of being a cruel businessman, trying to exploit a poor widow and her sister and of deceiving them by referring to trade secrets which didn't exist. In fact he had never said there were any trade secrets, just one or two tricks of the trade he didn't wish to reveal until they had completed the deal.

We all knew Father was in the right, as did his lawyer, but, with the ladies now playing the poor widow-card, things were turning nasty. It was threatening to become emotional, and this would be a drain on Father's health. Here the family doctor played a decisive part, saying that if the case went to court Father probably would not emerge in good enough condition to start a new life in Canada. My sister Pat bravely volunteered to be the conciliator, agreeing with the opposing solicitors to pay the ladies' money back, while I was making ornaments with renewed vigour to cover the household expenses.

Meanwhile Father's dream of moving to Canada received another blow when he was recalled to Canada House to have his eyesight checked. Pat says this was because when Father went for his original interview he failed to notice a piece of paper falling from the desk. Now he was told that, while the rest of the family were allowed to go the Canada, he could follow us only when we had proved we were financially secure. This of course was quite unacceptable to everyone, so we called the whole thing off.

The bungalow where we had lived for nearly twenty years had to be sold, but even when it had gone we were still in debt, which was a desperately distressing experience for as independently-minded a man as my father. He was now well past normal retirement age. His eyesight, indeed his health in general, was now deteriorating noticeably as a result of these set-backs and it seemed unlikely that he would ever be able to support his family again. My mother, who in normal circumstances would have been well able to support the family, was now totally committed to looking after her husband. Pat and I found ourselves the breadwinners, while John of course was still at school and badly in need of some kind of domestic stability. Our new economic circumstances did put pressure on the family for a while, and I believe it was only the closeness of our relationship, fostered by our parents from early on, which kept us together in the long run.

We were now living in rented rooms at no 144 Coldharbour Lane, a busy main road between Brixton and Camberwell, in a house owned by some stage friends of Father's. It was a grim contrast to our spacious accommodation in leafy Worcester Park. We had two rooms, each about 12 foot square, on the second floor, with a gas cooker on the landing. We had the use of the bathroom on the first floor but had to share it with two sets of tenants who lived on that level. Of these three friendly high-spirited Irish lads are the ones I remember most clearly. The owners of the house occupied the ground floor and basement. We had paraffin fires and square carpets with lino around the edges, as many people did in those days.

Pat and Mother slept in one room, which became the living-room by day, while the boys, Father, John and I, shared the other. In the early days Father was fit enough to climb the stairs, but he could hardly see anything, which in one sense was a mercy for him in these dingy surroundings. He carried a white stick and, with help, he could make his way to the pub called The Enterprise opposite. When he became more frail he spent most of his time in bed. A kind lady from the Royal National Institute for the Blind called at regular intervals, bringing materials for him to make baskets and stools from seagrass. Father would start them to please her, but he soon tired of such mundane tasks and Pat or I would have to complete them so as not to disappoint his visitor.

For this princely mansion it fell to Pat and me to pay the rent. On top of this Pat, then doing clerical work for an office in the City, was having to make weekly payments to the old ladies' solicitors. For myself, I was still trying to make garden ornaments, but without the benefit of our old workshop. I had rented a workshop, a sort of warehouse with a toilet and sink but no electricity, near the old one in Worcester Park, and for a while I commuted from there to Brixton on a small motorbike, a second-hand 250cc BSA paid for in weekly instalments.

Initially Mother had arranged for me to stay in Worcester Park with Mr and Mrs Weallans in Longfellow Road. This was conven-ient for my work, but for a young fellow of 22 it was rather restricting, as I often wanted to work late, sometimes all night. On the other hand I didn't want to contribute to the overcrowding in Coldharbour Lane. So without telling anyone I moved into the workshop, living in damp, cold conditions which seemed comfort-able by Army standards, but which became the despair of Mother. When she eventually found out, she immediately ordered me to Coldharbour Lane and looked for a workshop in Camberwell for me to use.

Moving out of the Weallans' house into the workshop was the start of my habit of all-night working, something that was to become quite normal for me for a few years. When I worked all night I would get up late in the morning, arising from the lino-covered flat table I used as my bed, rolling my blankets in plastic sheeting, and turning it into my work bench. Away from people I could work at night without disturbing anyone except the night-patrol policeman. Sometimes he would hear my shovel mixing cement and come to make sure it was me. This was the signal for me to stop and make us both a cup of tea.

Without electricity I relied on candles, very tiring to work with because the shadows were always moving, and later a hurricane lamp. I bought a Tilly pressure stove, a bucket and a bowl so that I could wash standing over a floor drain. I also had a frying pan, a saucepan for meals and a kettle for much-needed cups of tea. With no windows, just a skylight, it might sound like a prison, but to me it offered self-containment and privacy. My social life centred on Tony's Milk Bar where I would often spend an hour or two in the evening to give myself a break before starting again. As a parent myself I can now see why Mother didn't regard this as the ideal environment for her son, but at the time I was perfectly happy.

One problem I did have was that the workshop was some distance from the road. Whenever a truck came with a delivery of sand, usually five or six yards at a time, it simply dumped it in the road leaving me to cart it away with a wheelbarrow, which was hot and tedious work for one man working alone. I also found that many of the moulds needed replacing, a laborious business when I should have been making ornaments or even selling them. The seeds of my eventual downfall were probably already sown, but I carried on like a man obsessed, knowing I was the only person who could keep Father's business alive.

6

How to Make a Major's Garden Ornament

Father was always very careful not to reveal the secrets he had learned over many years of making garden gnomes, ducks, herons, hippopotami and suchlike. Why should he talk about these things? It was hard-earned information like this, after all, that gave him the cutting edge over his competitors. If there was one thing that really infuriated the old ladies who wanted to buy the business off him, it was his reference to 'trade secrets'. They felt they had been deceived by some masonic conspiracy, but of course it was never like that.

Father's ways of making garden ornaments can now be revealed without any great risk of anyone trying to copy them, because the whole business would be far too laborious for anyone living in the 1990s. Compared with the specialised skills of today's business-man, Father looks like something of a Renaissance man. He had to design his product, make it and then market it, all of this in working conditions which haven't been seen in south London since Dickens's day.

First one starts with a model. Nearly all the models were made by Father, though Pat proved herself very capable in this depart-ment later on. As I never matched their artistic skills in sculpture, I tended to restrict my design work to bird baths, shrub tubs and that sort of thing. Father usually made his models of white china clay, but quite often he would adapt an existing animal, removing undercuts which might catch when removing the mould. For tall slender birds such as herons he would often add reeds or rocks between the legs, partly for additional strength but partly to allow the cement to fill the mould.

Then the surface of the model was prepared, nice and smooth, making sure there were no awkward bits sticking out. Then we would make the mould, sometimes in plaster, sometimes in cement or even wood. These were always in sections so that they could be removed from the cast once it had set. To an unfamiliar eye these moulds looked totally baffling before they were assembled, like three-dimensional jigsaw puzzles.

For the more complicated figures the moulds were partly filled before the complete figure was assembled. Father used string to hold the moulds together, but I once had a stupid accident while cutting the string with the American army machete my father picked up on the air base in Norfolk, instead of with a knife as I should have done. I sliced the top of one finger in two, next to the bone. I called Mother, and she called Mrs Swain next door and they called the doctor, who stitched it up in his surgery. Nowadays, of course, you'd be sent to hospital, but that's what doctors did in those days. After this, always improvising, I found we could use instead of string half-inch wide strips of rubber from the inner tubes of lorries.

To make a mould we first had to decide on the sections. They had to lock together so that they didn't fall in on themselves while being filled. On the other hand they had to come away without catching when the cement was dry. We treated the inside surface of the mould to protect it, and the first thing we always made, in case it proved a popular line, was a plaster master-copy so that we could make a new mould in due course.

Father's usual mixture for garden ornaments was three to one or two-and-a-half to one – sand to cement, that is – depending on the shape of the finished product. Father always insisted on mixing it thoroughly by hand, and then putting it through a fine zinc riddle to remove even the tiniest of stones. Water was added from a can with a very fine rose, turning the mixture with a shovel all the time. This was easy enough when there were two of us, but it became a bit of a bind when I was on my own.

The test of whether the cement was wet enough was that, when you took a handful and squeezed, it should stay in a ball. If it produced streaks when you drew a float across the surface it was too wet, which was always a pain because you had to make up some more dry mix. It was worth taking the trouble to get the mixture right to avoid the cement sticking to the mould or leaving gaps which had to be patched up later. Far too much of my time was spent correcting any faults when the mould was removed. You filled the mould by tamping the cement down with a rod, taking care not to do this too energetically or you would damage the mould.

Twenty-four hours later you removed the mould with a wooden mallet. You then applied a finish of ground stone powder, the stone yard equivalent of sawdust which when dry makes a choking cloud of dust. Mixed with water this has the consistency of masonry paint, which is used to coat the cast giving colour and texture to the ornament. If you add extra cement you also have a paste which is very handy for small repairs, such as to the noses of garden gnomes.

You apply this stuff liberally but smoothly with a large soft brush, then cover with a damp cloth and leave it to set. You need a second or even a third coat, but in each case, to get a bond, you do this when the previous one is set but not quite dry.

After this comes the really messy bit, for which rubber gloves, plastic aprons, gum boots and any old clothes you can find are required. This is the antiquing process, using mineral black or commercial manganese dioxide, a ferocious substance which can eat into your skin if it is unprotected. It always seemed a pity, and indeed rather fraudulent, to smother a nice clean new figure with this dreadful concoction, but this is what you have to do to make it look old. The secret of success was timing: you had to wash it off again before it ate too deeply into the cement. You could always add another coat if you hadn't put enough on, but there was very little you could do once you had overdone it. With a sponge and water we would wipe the finished statue down, washing off the highlights but leaving shaded bits in the hollows. To pass Tom Major's inspection a good ornament needed to have a subtle shading – none of those harsh smudgy highlights you see in modern garden ornaments – otherwise it found itself on the scrap heap destined to be used as hard core for a building site. It is hardly surprising, therefore, that my father was upset when he found that a man who was buying this hard core was actually selling the reject figures at a higher price than the good ones were fetching.

Some objects weren't given the antiquing treatment because they were going to be painted all over. Ducks had to have eyes and beaks, the latter shaded with yellow at the tip and orange at the back. Dogs, cats and squirrels needed noses, eyes, whiskers and expressions around the eyes. Scotties had to have tartan collars, and a fully painted gnome required shading in the creases of his coat and hat, and on the rock he was sitting on. Crocodiles had big red mouths and thousands of little white teeth. One thing that shouldn't be overlooked, and it may a be a bit late to be saying this now, is that all these creatures required reinforcing wires: rabbits for their ears, ducks for their necks, and crocodiles for their tails.

The work ranged from fiddly to back-breaking and was always dirty. A bird bath encased in its plaster cast would seem to weigh a ton and yet had to be turned over to remove the mould. Constant contact with wet cement wore the skin off the tips of my fingers and broke my finger nails. The cement seemed to get into my blood, as well as into my hair, finger nails, clothes and everything else. I was always lifting and carrying things. Looking back, I think I must have been extremely fit.

6. How to Make a Major's Garden Ornament

Unlike many people's jobs, it was always satisfying. At the end of the day when I was packing prior to despatch, I could look at a shelf full of garden ornaments that resembled an animal army on the move, all of them made from start to finish by me. Looking at garden centres and their catalogues these days I am always seeing ornaments almost identical in design to the ones my father devised, but mostly very inferior in their manufacture.

7

National Service

Father had obtained a six-month deferment to my National Service on the grounds that I was essential to his business but eventually my departure could be delayed no longer. Not that I was complaining, mind you, because I knew I had to do my National Service sometime and I was getting tired of garden ornaments. My friends Eddie Scammel and John Colley, who had already been called up, had said it wasn't too bad.

One day in late 1950 I was in the back garden blacking the ornaments to give them the antique effect. It was my least favourite job, and I was covered in this filthy black stuff standing out in the open ground with a bitter wind blowing behind the greenhouse where my father had grown all his green tomatoes. I had lined up the ornaments on a marble table where they had frozen to the spot, and I had to fetch a bucket of hot water not only to free them but to loosen up my fingers and bring them back to life.

Just then I heard footsteps and my mother was saying: 'There's someone to see you, Terry.' It was my friend Eddie, resplendent in his Army uniform with a brilliant white lanyard over his shoulder and a grin to match.

'What's it like, Eddie?' I said.

'Not too bad,' he replied, giving me a look and then changing the subject.

Although Eddie wasn't exactly enthusiastic about the military life, I felt it might be worth a try.

In fact, of course, I had no option because in January 1951 my call-up papers arrived. I was to do my National Service, that saviour of bad boys and maker of good men, whether I liked it or not. I'm not sure how much I benefited from this experience, though it certainly made me more self-reliant, but in the next few months I saw some people whom it barely touched.

The Army was my third choice. Like most involuntary recruits, it seems, I opted first for the Navy and then for the Air Force.

'Sorry, quota filled,' they snapped in both cases when I went to see them for my medical and interview.

Even when I agreed to join the Army, they seemed doubtful about whether they really required my services.

'Now we do have room there,' the man said, 'at least in some parts.'

'Well, I'd rather like to learn something useful while I'm in the Army,' I said, perhaps optimistically. 'So I rather thought of the REME.'

'I'm sorry, that's full,' the interviewer barked. 'Everyone wants that.'

'Well, how about the Medical Corps?' I continued.

'We might be able to fit you in there if we hurry,' he said briskly, but softening up a little. 'Any special reason for suggesting the RAMC?'

I began to describe how, seven years previously, Mother had nearly died giving birth to my baby brother and that John's life, too, would surely have been lost if it hadn't been for the loving care of the doctors and nurses at the hospital. I had been deeply moved by this experience, I explained, and longed to be able to give something back to the medical profession. This was all true.

And so it was, with John's unwitting assistance, that I joined the Medics, while most of my friends went into the infantry to spend their time 'digging ruddy holes and marching up and down'.

There was quite enough meaningless parade ground routine

even in the Medical Corps, I soon discovered, when I reported as instructed with my call-up papers to the Army School of Health at Mytchett near Aldershot.

This was the first time in my life that I had been away from home and from Mother's loving attention, and I found myself in the care of some of some officers who, it honestly seemed to me, needed to have their heads examined. Their first trick was to give us some Army webbing with the brass painted black, telling us they wanted the brass all shiny by the next morning. The second task was to take some brown officers' boots and have them dyed black. I am a reasonably practical person and the only assumption I could make was that half of everything you did in the Army was a waste of time, and that some of the people in command were completely barmy. I hate to think what a more sensitive person would have made of it.

After two weeks of such basic essentials, marching up and down, cleaning our kit and suffering humiliation in silence, we were judged fit to go to the Queen Elizabeth Barracks, home of the RAMC in Ash Vale near Aldershot. With customary bloody-mindedness, which would get you nowhere in civilian life, the truck driver parked in such a way that we all had to jump down into a puddle. Here we lived in wooden huts that had been condemned many years before and did drill, and more drill, with a little medical training as light relief. I have no sense of rhythm and it always seemed to me that I was the only one in time in our squad.

All the same the entire squad passed out quite well, and by 1st May I was now ready for posting abroad. First there was time for a last visit to my family, and I can remember that just as I was leaving I was standing by the gate with my kit bag over my shoulder and my case in my hand when Mother called me back to the front door. There were tears in her eyes as she prepared to make a solemn announcement.

'Terry,' she said. 'Promise me something.'

'Of course, Mother,' I replied. 'Anything you like.'

'Please don't go with any German girls while you're over there.'

That's my fun curtailed, I thought, because I always kept my promises with my mother.

Ten days later we sailed from Harwich to the Hook of Holland where, perhaps as a result of Mother's strictures, my main impression of the transit depot was the Dutch women. They all looked so well-scrubbed, so pink and shiny. We were very well looked after, fed and watered, by these pristine ladies, before bedding down for what was, for me, my first night outside England.

After a couple of days we were assembled in front of a platform full of officers and told that the medics were over-subscribed in the nursing grade although still needed in the clerical grade – just my luck, I thought. We were told our record cards would be picked out at random and our names and numbers called out. If the person chosen was clerical the card would go back in the box. If he was in the nursing section he would be transferred to the infantry. I waited with fingers tightly crossed.

Then my name was called and I walked slowly to the platform. Endless vistas of muddy trenches and wet parade grounds, with no useful experience gained from them, swam through my brain when my turn came to stand in front of the clerk next to the sergeant major.

'Name and number,' said the clerk.

'Private 294 Major-Ball T., sir,' I replied in my firmest voice, realising this was my moment to tell the story about John and Mother once again. 'Excuse me, sir.'

'Yes, what is it?' said the sergeant major.

'Is there any chance of being transferred back later?' enquired Major-Ball T.

'Why?' said the sergeant major, giving me a strange stare.

I explained how I was deeply moved by my mother's and my brother's lives being saved by the devotion and care of the nurses, and how I would like the opportunity of repaying my debt to the community and indeed to the medical world. The sergeant major, who had obviously not heard anything like this before, looked at me with an experienced eye and began to smile. I had never seen a sergeant major smile.

'Will you have a word with this man?' he said to the major sitting next to him.

Once again I told the story about John and Mother. This time, after some conferring between the clerk and the major, they crossed my name out and told me to go and sit at the back of the hall. Never in the history of human conflict has a private soldier been so relieved. There was some muttering at the back of the hall about what had been said but, as Father would say, that was a trade secret.

On 16 May I was transferred to the 30th Field Ambulance at Bad Lippspringe and assigned to No 1 Casualty Collecting Post and installed in some barracks which I was told were built as a sanatorium and later used by the SS. This seemed quite plausible because the grounds were attractive – with trees, grass, bushes, a well-kept lawn, gravel paths and a brook running through the middle. The buildings didn't have the usual depressing air of a military institution.

There wasn't much nursing because we only had mock casualties and my main task in the camp was helping to run the dining hall, serving food and clearing up afterwards. We had the occasional lecture. It was quite a pleasant life. On training schemes I was in charge of an ambulance, usually with a driver who spoke very little English, and quite early on this was to get me into trouble.

One scorching hot day we were cruising around in the ambulance, not talking much because of the language problem. I think I must have been in a sleepy, muggy sort of stupor because I failed to notice that he was trying to tell me something. 'Burning,' he was saying, 'Fire.'

'Yes,' I said sleepily. Then I looked out of the window and saw that the ambulance was indeed burning. The whole of the side was a mass of flames. He jumped out of the cab, grabbed the fire extinguisher and eventually put out the flames, but there was a very large hole in the canvas covering and the wooden framework was badly charred. Sergeant Stapleton warned me solemnly that I would be for the high jump for this, but the official report cleared me, saying that the camouflage netting had been attached to the exhaust pipe by the people in the transport pool and the very hot weather, helped by the wind, had done the rest.

Shortly afterwards I followed this with two *faux pas* in one day. I had been sent with a few others to help a staff officer move house. The officer's wife was a nice lady who gave us tea and cakes even before we started. We were assembling a large wardrobe in sections and my job was to sit inside, pushing the pieces into place while they screwed them together. Perhaps because of the cakes, perhaps because it was very stuffy inside the cupboard, I fell asleep and the others thought it would be a fine joke to leave me there when they left. When I woke up I had to explain to the startled lady why I was still in her bedroom, and I also had to make my way back to the barracks several miles away, lost and without any German money and without being able to speak German.

I saw a large khaki car and put my hand up. This was my second *faux pas*. The corporal at the wheel was not pleased to see me. When I explained my embarrassing predicament he swore at me to jump in the back with the parcels but to keep my head down. As we swept through the gates of the barracks I saw the guard turn out and wondered why. The corporal swore at me again, for not keeping my head down. 'It's a good job I know that guard corporal,' he said. When he dropped me at my block my own corporal came out and addressed me with a very rude and pointed remark. I was then told to get inside, and my punishment was to spend the evening washing the floor of the corridor and toilets. To my way of thinking this was a rare opportunity in the army to do something useful, instead of sitting around in the canteen and polishing the soles of one's boots. It was only afterwards that I found out what my misdemeanor had been – the car I had hitched a lift in was the Brigadier's car and the guard corporal at the gate had been saluting the car.

By and large army life was uneventful. We had no NAAFI in our unit and most people spent their time drinking German beer or playing darts. I preferred to go into town, a short walk through the woods, to the cinema, the YMCA, or the sausage shop, but not the bars. I even spoke to a few young ladies, which I hope did not contravene Mother's decree, for the chatty ladies were behind the counter at the YMCA and were too advanced in years to be described as girls. There was a shortage of female company in the camp, and whenever word got around that the nursing sisters were sunbathing on the lawn nearby all the men would go that way to the barracks.

I spent more than my share of my time in the Medical Corps as a patient, which I like to think gives me a special insight into their work. On one occasion I had an ingrowing toenail removed without an anaesthetic while I was held down by several beefy German nurses. Another time I had an infected wisdom tooth, but while I was in the ward I got tonsillitis as well. I remember the man in the next bed, who had just had all his teeth out, being very annoyed that my operation had produced more blood on the pillow than his had. I also discovered the terrors of being carried downstairs on a stretcher. The worst thing is when they pick up the stretcher to pass it over the bends. This was easily my most dangerous exploit in the army, should my grandchildren ever ask me.

I went home on my first leave loaded with presents for everyone and a selection of German comics for John. I had bought the comics on the station and stuffed them, with some fruit for the journey, in my battledress tunic. This raised the suspicions of the customs men, who summoned me into their office and told me to remove my jacket. They seemed rather annoyed that my explanation was genuine and tried to charge me £1 10s duty on a watch I had bought for Mother. This would have made John's German comics a most expensive piece of literature, but eventually the customs men chalked my case and let me go.

My army days came to a sudden end when I returned from the YMCA one night at 10pm to be told to report to the guard house. This was usually a sign of trouble, although as far as I knew I hadn't done anything wrong. They told me without explanation to pack my bags and prepare for a transfer. Early next morning, saying my goodbyes, I realised I had made a lot of friends in the army and was sorry to see the last of them.

At the orderly office I was told that I was being discharged on compassionate grounds and sent back to the Military Hospital in Cambridge. Then I was taken by truck to the nearest station and from there by train to the Hook of Holland. My discharge and return home should have been a cause for celebration and I bought half a bottle of brandy at the station to keep me warm on deck but, in the absence of any explanation, I was becoming increasingly worried that some terrible disaster had befallen my family.

When I got home I found my father's health had taken a turn for the worse and that was why I was being discharged, but I still had three months with the Medical Corps in Aldershot and a further 36 months on the Supplementary Reserve. I am pleased to say that my discharge papers said my military conduct was very good, and described me as trustworthy. I had done my best to be the kind of soldier Father and Mother could be proud of. Certainly I was proud of my Corps and I loved to walk out in my maroon lanyard and maroon-and-navy dress cap.

One thing I learned in the Medical Corps was that I wasn't destined to be a soldier or a nurse. I was too much of an individual to obey orders without question, which is highly dangerous in battle. And I was far too deeply affected by death and suffering ever to be a nurse. They may seem strange bedfellows, soldiers and nurses, but each plays a part in the British Army.

Life at home was becoming more and more of a struggle and it wasn't long before I discovered that the army wasn't such a hassle after all. However, I would have put up with anything to be back with the family.

8

Jack the Lad

Although I don't think National Service affected my outlook as much as it did some people's, it does seem to have been a watershed in my life, particularly in terms of friendships. Many of my old friends had found new acquaintances and interests, others had simply left home. Even the neighbours, Mr and Mrs Cowley and their daughter Noreen (who used to share the air raid shelter), had moved to run a pig farm while I was away and there were new people next door. Noreen, who used to pester me in the workshop with 'Can I fill the moulds, Terry?', came over to welcome me home, but I was held up at the barracks and we had only about an hour to chat before I had to walk her to the station. Apart from one visit to their farm a few months later it was to be forty years before I saw her again. The Sargent family had also moved, but I've been lucky and recently made contact with one of their daughters and her husband, who have invited us to stay. Mrs Brand had also moved to the country and I recently saw her and her daughter Joan when we had a quiet lunch in a country pub and a walk around her grounds. It was the same story with many other friends from that part of Longfellow Road, though in the last few years I have caught up with many of them and received a warm welcome. I remember the first few months after my return as rather lonely.

Two years ago I met many old friends at the Diamond Wedding of Mr and Mrs Scott, including their two daughters, Sonia and Angela. My contemporaries had now become adults and many of them had children of their own. It was some time before I made contact with Eddie Scammell and John Carey, both from Long-fellow Road, and I learned that John Colley had died. It was with John that I had bicycled to Littlehampton two years before I joined the army. This was a foolhardy expedition because neither of us had cycled more than five miles before, and our legs ached for days afterwards.

I wasn't a great cinema-goer, which was the key to social success in those days, partly because it cost money, and that was in short supply. Instead I used to spend my spare evenings walking up and down Worcester Park High Street looking in shop windows and making what visits I could afford to Toni's Milk Bar. Here I met my first dream girl. She had jet-black hair and worked in Timothy Whites the Chemists, and she had a blonde friend. One day I plucked up courage and asked her out. 'Perhaps,' she said myste-riously. Encouraged by her response, I spent all my money on two dozen carnations, twelve white and twelve red. When I gave them to her she laughed at me. I later heard she didn't even take them home but gave them to the church.

It was at Toni's Milk Bar that I met Ted Hunt. We liked each other and I invited him home, where he got on famously with Mother, who gave him a big supper. Ted was living with two other boys at home although his parents were away. So when Mother decided it was too late for him to go home, she said he was to sleep on the settee for the night. Next morning when I got up I found that Ted was missing, as indeed was Mother. It transpired that she had taken him to Sutton to buy a bunk bed.

'Ted will be staying for a while,' Mother announced imperiously when they got back. Well, he certainly did. He stayed until he got married about a year later. We became good friends and we had a lot of fun together. Ted had a small Ford car and an eye for the girls. Long before he met his wife Leonie we both darted about in that car. At weekends he would splash out and hire a white Ford

Consul or Zephyr, whichever was the latest model, from Godfrey Davis.

Occasionally on Saturday nights we would play Jack the Lad and go to the Kingston Empire, hiring a box between the two of us with two girls if we were lucky, and sometimes we also had a cigar, mainly for effect. Sometimes we would drive down to Hastings to see a waitress who worked at the Seagull Café, just for a chat – it was all innocent fun in those days. On other nights and on Sunday mornings we went to Toni's Milk Bar in Worcester Park or the Laskedene in North Cheam, and it was here that we met Veronica, or Ronnie as we called her, and her sister whose name I forget. The same crowd went to both places which were the favoured night spots for us in those days.

The usual story with girls was that Ted would get the slim glamorous one and I would get the plainer, tubbier one. I have no complaints about this because in my experience the latter type is jollier and more entertaining. Ronnie was certainly a lovely girl and a bundle of fun. One night we were taking the girls home much later than their allotted time. We knew we were in trouble and, sure enough, there was their mother waiting on the doorstep, so we dropped the girls off quickly before their mother could reach us. On the way home we were pondering whether we would ever be allowed to see the girls again when I had an idea. Next morning at seven we took the car to the workshop and loaded the boot with a three-piece fountain, one of my most expensive garden ornaments. We coasted down the hill to Ronnie's house, quietly stopped outside, then tip-toed across the front garden and set the fountain up in the centre of the lawn. We knocked on the door and stood back. I am happy to report that the fountain had the desired effect on the girls' mother, who opened the door and rushed across the lawn to admire my handiwork. We were given a solemn warning to get the girls home on time, followed by tea and toast.

Over the years Ted and I calmed down a bit after he met Leonie, who lived in Greenford in north-west London. There was a lot of travelling back and forth between north and south. Then we used to go out as a threesome. If I said I was getting in their way they would insist I went along with them. They were great times, with a lot of laughter. At some point Ted exchanged the black Ford for a motorbike and I got one too, although I had to give it back when I fell behind on the payments.

Mother shed a few tears when Ted left our bungalow on the day of his marriage. I was his best man, as he was later to be mine. On his wedding morning, relaxed as ever, Ted arrived home late after having his hair done and we had to rush across London to get to St Barnabas Church in Northolt. We could see the bride's car approaching as we arrived and we leapt out of our van, putting our jackets on as we ran to the church.

When I first knew Ted he worked for Lyons the caterers delivering to their factory and tea shops – he got to know Leonie because she worked on the exchange at Lyons Greenford factory. Later we both worked for Decca Records making the old 78 rpm discs. In the early days he always tried his best to find me a suitable girl, but I don't think I was ready for marriage at that stage – the only girl I might have married at around that time eventually gave up waiting for me to make up my mind and went to live in New Zealand. After we moved to Coldharbour Lane Ted still visited us but we lost touch after the move to Burton Road. I haven't seen him for about 30 years, although I think I may have spotted him on a television news report at the time of the floods in Chichester in March 1994. If anyone can put me back in touch with him I would be very grateful.

9

Woolworths and Shirley

During the mid-fifties things weren't running smoothly for Major's Garden Ornaments. Orders were down and the equipment was badly in need of replacement, making the work even more laborious than it should have been. I had to file off the protruding edges of the concrete figures where the moulds didn't fit together properly and had no time at all for selling. None of the family was in a position to do much to improve the situation. Father was now too ill to work and Mother, who was usually the driving force, particularly on the sales side, when he was indisposed, was compelled to stay at home to look after him. Her health was also declining, and John of course was still at school.

My sister Pat and I therefore found ourselves as the main breadwinners, not just trying to keep the business going but actually supporting the family. Pat by now had left art school, and her skills were much in demand at Major's Garden Ornaments, but only on a part-time basis because she had her own career. As for myself, I had now spent so much time trying to keep the business going that I didn't feel like giving in to adversity. My father and headmaster had tried to persuade me to train for a trade when I left school but I had refused. Garden ornaments were to be my life. Now they were proved right, for I wasn't qualified to do anything else. This was the predicament I found myself in now that things had gone wrong.

At one point in desperation I took a job in a plastics moulding company in Mitcham, near Wimbledon. The work was unbelievably tedious most of the time, with occasional bursts of serious aggravation. I was part of a team testing the material at regular intervals as it spewed out of the machines and, although it was scarcely our fault when it fell below the standards of excellence required of the finished product, the testers were always the ones who took the blame for shoddy workmanship by the rest of the team. I used to travel to Mitcham from Brixton by motorbike – and there lies another sad tale. When I fell behind with the payments and was forced to take the bike back to the shop, I had to use the bus and tube, as indeed I have ever since. Mother hated me doing this job, largely I think because of the smell of my clothes when I got home each evening. Though she would never say anything so impolite, it was as if they were subjected to the constant attention of a particularly active neighbourhood tom cat. She would make me take off my outer clothes and leave them in a plastic bag on the landing outside the flat ready for my less than elegant departure the next morning. I have often wondered what the neighbours thought I did, smelling like that. All I can say is that my family was lucky I didn't work in the grinding department at the plastics factory. These poor men would come into the test room covered from head to foot in coloured powder, apart from rings round their mouths and eyes where their masks and goggles had been. After six months I was made redundant, but not before I had learned a valuable lesson in race relations.

It had been a long hot day at the factory and everyone was irritable. The millers and grinders worked on a bonus system and consequently suffered when the weather affected the quality of the material they were milling, so that they missed their targets and their earnings were reduced. They nearly always blamed us, the testers, on these occasions, seldom themselves. Towards the end of the day I was overcome by a splitting headache. I felt sick, and my head was spinning when I left the factory for my journey home. I remember clutching some iron railings and watching the millers and grinders, the very people I spent my time trying to help, hurrying past. Then one of the black labourers stopped and asked me what was wrong. He took me on the underground to my usual station and put me on the bus, telling the conductor where to drop me off. There weren't many black people in south London in those days and I wasn't familiar with West Indians. He was a perfect gentleman and I will always remember him.

After a further six months struggling along in the family business I resolved next time to look for a job with better prospects. So when I saw an advertisement for trainee managers for Woolworths in Brixton, I applied for one of these positions. Rather to my surprise, because self-confidence wasn't one of my strong points at that time, I was given a job. The money wasn't great, but it was a steady income, a good deal more reliable than the income the family firm then provided. It also meant that I would receive some management training. What I didn't know at the time was that it was the most important decision I have made in my life, but for a very special reason. It was at Woolworths that I was to meet my wife Shirley.

The idea of being trained as a manager of Woolworths filled me with trepidation. I had never worked in a shop before, and Woolworths in those days was some shop. These were the days before self-service and prepackaging when, if you wanted a quarter of mixed sweets, they would be individually selected for you by an obliging assistant. You could buy loose biscuits, pointing to the tin you liked, and pieces of cake sliced as you directed. Nothing was wasted even then, twelve years after the war, and if you were hard up you could buy a bag of broken biscuits. This was the heyday of Woolworth stores when customers were courted and served with speed, not left to potter around looking for obscure items which the staff don't even know about before standing in a long queue at the cash desk.

The manager, Mr Hazeldene, ran the Brixton store, known as Metropolitan 7, with a rod of iron. He was often at odds with the area supervisor not because of his commercial acumen which was considerable – Mr Hazeldene was paid partly on percentage rates, so he usually met his targets and often surpassed them – but because when it came to staff relations he was a little short on charm. There was little in the way of employment legislation, and managers didn't treat their staff with kid gloves as they do now. Mr Hazeldene was king of all the counters he surveyed. All too often I saw one of the girls being taken upstairs to his office by the staff supervisor, only to come down a little later with her coat on, never to be seen in the store again.

Mercifully, I didn't cross swords with him at first because, as a new recruit, my first job was in the stockroom, which was the domain of the storekeeper, Mr Baker. This strange character wore a brown warehouse coat and a permanent grin to match – his teeth were deeply stained by chain-smoking – but probably the most astonishing thing about him was his memory. Biscuits were stacked by the ton, but there was always an untidy pile of smaller parcels, like an immovable mountain, near the packing bench. Lesser mortals would look with terror at this heap and quite often, when the downstairs lady-supervisors would ask for a particular parcel, he would brush their enquiries aside, saying they just had to wait until it was unpacked. This would provoke the ladies to attack the pile themselves, but he would have nothing of this – the pile would be disturbed, it could lead to disorder. Thus galvanised into action, he would dive headlong into the centre of the heap like a ferret and retrieve the parcel on demand with the minimum of disruption and delay.

My first opportunity to venture outside the stockroom came at Christmas time when they needed someone downstairs to sell Christmas trees. The trees came in three different sizes, in bundles of ten. I was responsible for setting them out and it gave me some scope for salesmanship. I was able to make sure a little old lady in a ragged coat got good value for her money while seeing that the one in the fur bought the dearest. It appealed to my social conscience. Dashing from side to side of my little pitch like a market trader, I began to think I had missed my calling in life. I dare say there are a few snobs in the media who would have had some fun if the Prime Minister's brother had been a market trader, but I really enjoyed being a salesman, meeting the extraordinary cross-section of people who lived in Brixton at that time.

After Christmas I was back in the stockroom, but my experience selling trees meant that I had met some of the staff on the sales floor, particularly some charming young ladies. One of them, a Saturday girl with a lovely nature, was the daughter of a senior officer at Brixton prison. Sadly he was later transferred to another prison and the family went too. There was also Pearl, a blonde girl who sold ice-cream in Woolworths by day and at the Astoria cinema by Brixton police station in the evenings. I used to go to the Astoria several times a week and, unlike my brother John who watched films such as *The Flame* and *The Arrow* several times until he knew them by heart without ever falling asleep, I must confess I tend to nod off when I've seen a film a couple of times. My blonde friend began to realise this, and if she saw me asleep she would open my fingers and put an ice-cream tub in my hand. I would see her smile gleaming in the dark, laughing at me as the coldness of the ice-cream tub woke me up.

After the show I would walk Pearl home to Peckham, a distance of several miles, walking and talking and holding hands. This may sound like the ultimate gesture of devotion. There may have been the occasional kiss, but I don't think so. It was a platonic friendship. At least I thought it was at the time, but after a few months she suddenly put an end to it. I have since wondered since whether Pearl really wanted a more serious relationship, but at the time I was innocently unaware of this. Perhaps I was unfair to her. At any rate I have never forgotten her.

There was also Ruth, the Irish usherette at the cinema in Camberwell Green who knew the two young Irishmen who lived in the same house as us in Coldharbour Lane. I used to walk Ruth home too, but I knew she neither expected nor wanted anything more. Later she went back to Ireland, but she kept in touch even after I was married.

The truth is I was really rather frightened of girls but fascinated by them. I have already described how my mother solemnly warned me not to go with any German girls when I went to Germany to do my national service. On another occasion she told me that what sometimes passes for love is actually passion. Real love, she said, was for marriage. As a result of my mother's strictures, I have only told one girl that I loved her, and that was my wife. It follows that my brother, who had the same mother, must have much the same philosophy, which is why I regard with contempt the lurid conjecture in some magazines in recent years.

Girls were still high on my agenda at Woolworths at the beginning of 1958, although at that stage I hadn't yet met Shirley. Male and female staff were very much segregated in Woolworths in the fifties, indeed they had separate tables in the staff canteen. By this time I had started my management training on the shop floor, in a section which included the sweet counter. From here I had a much better vantage point than I had had in the stockroom. The two young ladies in the invoice office caught my eye early in 1958, one of them a blonde, the other a brunette, both of them under the stern eye of their redoubtable office manager Connie. The brunette wore high heels and walked with a brisk step, making a very distinctive sound. The urge to look up whenever I heard her coming was irresistible. I also began to find spurious excuses to visit the invoice office, investigating obscure customer enquiries. Such were the heady responsibilities of being on the shop floor that I no longer had to wait for Mr Baker, the storekeeper, to find a dubious invoice in the stockroom before I could visit the girls in the invoice department. I could go there more or less whenever I felt like it and the frequency of my visits hadn't gone unnoticed by Connie and by the delectable brunette in the invoice department, who was called Shirley. Both of them thought I was after Barbara, the blonde.

Before I could make myself known as well as I would have liked to either of the young ladies in the invoice department, I fell foul of Mr Hazeldene, the manager, and his strange lack of finesse in dealing with staff. Foolishly perhaps, I became involved in a discussion with the staff on the sweet counter, who were always complaining about a draught which they said was coming from a ventilation shaft overhead. The young ladies on the counters liked to bait the trainee managers, or floor walkers as they called us. I was trying to explain as diplomatically as I could that it was pointless complaining about this because the ventilation grill was boarded up in winter to prevent draughts. At this stage Mr Hazeldene appeared, biting his nails as he always did when he was in a rage and with his face flushed. Whenever he was in a temper he would shout insults at his floor walkers from several counters away, instead of asking them to his office. He would often bellow across the store without trying to find out what was really going on. In this instance he had got it badly wrong, accusing me of chatting up the girls on the sweet counter, when in fact I was doing some much-needed staff relations work on his behalf. He told me he had put me on the shop floor to work, and that if I was unable to do that I should get back to the stockroom where I came from.

I confess I do have a stubborn streak and I don't care to be patronised. I respect authority but I don't like to be put down. I give my word and I keep it, and I expect others to do the same. But on this occasion my uncompromising attitude led to my downfall as a trainee manager in Woolworths.

Instead of saying nothing as the others did, I walked over to Mr Hazeldene and told him what he could do with his sales floor, and his whole store as well if he cared to, adding that I would be in the stockroom if he wished to sack me. With that I returned to the stockroom from which I had so recently been promoted. I continued to work there and heard no more from Mr Hazeldene, so I have to say that he probably wasn't trying to get rid of me after all. In the canteen I had daily glimpses of the girls from the invoice department and frequently managed to find an excuse to visit them.

Life went drearily on in the stockroom, and then I began to notice that the Christmas trees were coming in again. A few days later the deputy manager, Mr Middup, came to see me to say that Mr Hazeldene wanted me to come downstairs and sell Christmas trees. Middup was a much easier man than Hazeldene. I got on well with him, in fact we used to travel home together on the same bus.

'I presume you're joking,' I said giving him one of my defiant stares. 'You go and tell Hazeldene he didn't like my work when I was on the floor so he sent be back up here. Now he thinks I'm going to come down and sell his Christmas trees. Well, he's got another think coming.'

'He's going to be very put out,' Mr Middup said sadly as he departed.

I got back to work on the unpacking bench.

Ten minutes later he was back. 'Hazeldene says you've got five minutes to come down and start selling Christmas trees,' he said in his flat I'm-not-getting-involved voice. 'Or else.'

'Or else what?' I said. Middup went away and I got on with my work.

This time he was back in five minutes. 'Sorry, Terry, he says if you're not down selling in five minutes you finish on Saturday.'

98

'Is that definite?' I said facing him, knowing I had forced a confrontation.

'That's it,' he said. 'Sorry, Terry, you know the old man.'

'Right,' I said. 'Tell him, thank you very much, I'll finish on Friday.'

'All right, if that's what you want,' he said, as he departed once more. 'But I'll be sad to see you go.'

Then he was back with another message from the great man. 'He says you can pick up your cards on Saturday,' he said with a tight grin which seemed to be saying how sorry he was.

'All right,' I said. 'Now I'll go down and sell his ruddy Christmas trees. But I'll have my tea first.'

As showdowns go, it may seem pretty pointless in retrospect. Why did I make such a fuss when I knew I enjoyed selling Christmas trees after all? I might have been a Woolworths manager, as many of my contemporary trainees subsequently became, if I hadn't had this quarrel with Hazeldene. I have mellowed with age, but in those days I had a low flash-point. I had made my point and retained my integrity but lost the argument – and my job. My brother John learned very early in his career how to avoid getting into a situation like this. He makes his point, retains his integrity and wins the argument. And he has to endure worse insults from his opponents than I did from the manager of Woolworths. As far as I was concerned I had no intention of obeying orders from a rude and unjust boss. Years later I met Mr Hazeldene when I went to Woolworths to find out about the wholesale cost of plastic soldiers – Father and I had seen some cheap moulding machines for manufacturing plastic soldiers and wanted to check the market – and I found that, now that I no longer worked for him, he was obliging and friendly. So why did I pick a fight with him? I have learned that some things in life just happen. There is nothing you can do to change them, however much you realise your whole career depended on a particular event. In any case, it was the argument with Hazeldene which led me to meet Shirley.

I sold all the Christmas trees by Thursday, two days before my time was up, and had just as good a time as I had the previous year. Then I realised that my window of opportunity was also diminishing as far as the young ladies in the invoice department were concerned. By Friday night I still hadn't summoned up the courage to ask Shirley to come out with me.

On Saturday morning, my last day at Woolworths, I knew it was now or never, and it had to be now because never was unthinkable. Palms perspiring, heart thumping, I approached the invoice department and went up to Connie.

'May I ask Shirley something?' I asked her.

'Yes,' she replied, rather to my surprise. Surely things weren't going to plan, I thought to myself. Shirley, who had heard my voice, looked around as I moved towards her, clearing my throat.

'A friend of mine has two tickets for the theatre at Streatham and he can't go,' I said bluntly, with no frills, no smooth patter at all. 'So he has given them to me. Would you like to come?'

Actually, this was a lie; there were no such tickets, but I was in a tight corner, having left everything until the last minute. Desperate needs require desperate measures. Even as I waited, apparently for an eternity, for Shirley to give her answer, I was calculating that I had only 15 minutes to spare before lunch, which was when I had planned to get the tickets.

Much to my relief Shirley said yes and, perhaps even more surprisingly, the tickets were available. We arranged to meet outside Brixton Town Hall, later to be the scene of John's early political successes, but that day it was a triumph in my life.

I shall always remember that night, waiting by the Town Hall as Shirley came towards me. It was snowing very slightly and she looked the most beautiful girl in the world. After the show we took the bus back to Brixton and walked slowly down Acre Lane to

Margate Road, where she lived with her parents. She stopped at the end of her road, the snow settling on her flimsy head-scarf. She said she had enjoyed herself and, yes, she would like another date. Then she was gone, running down the road to her house. There can't have been a happier man in the world. Woolworths was very far from my mind.

10

Back to Garden Ornaments

Christmas 1958 found me with a serious girlfriend but once again with no proper job. I returned to my garden ornaments, this time to a large order for Mr Spiers, one of our oldest regular customers. Recently I found a note in an old diary which shows that although Shirley wasn't complaining she was already resigned to my strange routine. The diary shows that I worked all night on New Year's Eve on Mr Spiers's order, and didn't come home until 5.30 am. Then I was back at the workshop at 9.30, waiting for Mr Spiers to collect his garden ornaments at 10.00. Mr Spiers must have paid me well, because the diary also says we went to the Brixton Astoria that night to see *The Two-headed Spy* and *Apache Territory*. I can only hope, after my previous night in the workshop, that I didn't snore too loudly, but if I did Shirley was too kind to comment. The next day I went to Shirley's house to meet her parents and a few days later she came to Coldharbour Lane to see mine for the first time. This shows that I must have decided almost immediately that she was the girl for me. The fact that we didn't get married for nearly two years simply indicates what dire financial straits the family was in at the beginning of 1959.

At the time I felt I couldn't get married because of the loss of income this would mean to my parents, and even after our wedding in September 1960 Shirley and I continued to pay them an allowance. Even when mother needed extra financial help Shirley never complained. Sadly our parents had died by the time John and Norma married in 1970, my mother only a fortnight before the wedding. My younger brother was as speedy as I was in realising that he had met the girl of his dreams, but he was able to marry her almost immediately. Early in 1959, however, life was very difficult for the family. My diary says there were constant visits from the doctor for my father or mother, while John, who was still at school, used to run errands to the chemist in Camberwell Green to buy pills. According to one entry, I brought the paraffin stove home from the workshop, a sure sign that Father was ill and business was slack. I see that I was offering discounts to favoured customers and that I was reduced to buying individual bags of cement at 7s 6d each. My finances must have been in a dreadful state because I was still making weekly payments on insurance stamps dating back to pre-Woolworths days and occasionally failing to have the money needed to run the house on time.

Then things began to look up. We received good orders from three regular customers, David's Rural Industries, Bentalls of Kingston and our old friend Mr Spiers of Cliftonville. I had to borrow five pounds to buy the sand and cement to make them. Thanks to these orders, and to Father receiving his cheque from the Variety Artists Benevolent Fund, we were suddenly solvent again. Mother had been writing to customers explaining that we were in trouble and might have to close down. Some of them had responded very generously, Mr Spiers with a £25 advance and later a £58 order.

These offers of help enabled us to continue in a shaky fashion, with Pat often assisting in the evenings. My mother, who could no longer cope with production work, often helped with the packing. She also visited Mr Spiers in Cliftonville and he offered to back us if were threatened with closure. My diary shows that I was still working absurd hours, often going back to the workshop after I had taken Shirley out in the evening. I was also helping out at home, mending shoes for myself and John, and even turning my younger brother's trousers up. John left school in March 1959, although he went back later to do exams. He got his first job, with Price Forbes accountants, in June but he wasn't happy and soon left. None of us wanted him to become as involved in the family firm as I had been, although later he did come and work with me in Camberwell.

Meanwhile there were other important developments in the family. Pat married Peter Dessoy, a baker. I gave the bride away and John was best man because Peter's brother was abroad on National Service. Shirley and I became engaged, the family firm was taken over by Commander David, one of our regular customers, and we all moved from Coldharbour Lane to a larger flat a mile away in Burton Road. Here for the first time since Father sold the bungalow in Worcester Park there was room for all of us, although John and I had to share a room. After Pat and Peter married and needed the room with the double bed, John and I had to move into a tiny room with bunk beds. Shirley, though living with her parents in Margate Road, already seemed very much part of the family. She was still working in Woolworths and visiting Mother at lunchtimes to keep an eye on her in Burton Road. John, who was becoming a dab hand with a frying pan, often cooked lunch for his mother and future sister-in-law.

I think we all felt rather sad moving from Coldharbour Lane. Though it was far from luxurious, we had certainly lived life to the full. The new flat was part of a house on a bend in the road, so that it was triangular with a broad frontage and a large front garden but nothing at all at the back. Unlike to Coldharbour Lane it had a downstairs dining-room, an underground larder, a kitchen and a cellar. Upstairs there was a lounge, a large bedroom and a very small one. There was also a medium-sized bedroom on the next floor. We had to share a bathroom with another flat but it had a coin-in-the-slot gas meter for heating the water, which seemed like luxury after our previous flat.

Shortly after we moved to Burton Road I hired a van and a driver and went with John to collect my mother's family furniture, which had been stored in an old workshop belonging to a local builder in Worcester Park. We found to our horror that it was riddled with woodworm, and we had to take it back to our own workshop and burn it. We were both worried that Mother might say we had done the wrong thing, but she took the bad news with equanimity, as she always did, saying we would just have to buy some new furniture. But how could we afford new furniture? We had already paid what seemed like a fortune for some new linoleum and curtains and I was having some trouble sorting out a complicated income tax bill. It was only because a friendly accountant from Worcester Park days agreed to sort out my financial affairs for nothing that I was able to remain solvent.

There were two other new inhabitants at Burton Road which Mother absorbed into the household apparently without turning a hair. The first was a jackdaw which John had found somewhere. It had mysteriously arrived in a friend's garden. It tells us something about the cordial relationship John enjoyed with his mother that he simply brought it home and assumed it would have a happy life. A man from the RSPCA told us that it was a domesticated bird and shouldn't be released into the wild, so we built a cage for it. It was certainly highly intelligent and began to collect shiny trinkets from around the house. It also became a remarkable mimic and used to imitate Mother's friend Mrs Dodd. Every time the door bell rang the bird would sing out: 'It's me, Gwen, I've arrived.' This was an early example of talent-spotting by the future Prime Minister.

The other newcomer to the household was a hamster named Christine. Father was now blind and spent most of his time in bed. He had a talking-book provided by the National Institute for the Blind, but in those days they consisted of gramophone records which had to be turned over at regular intervals. Although these

106

were designed to be used by the blind, Father never got the hang of his special player. He would simply yell for help when the record came to an end. It was in an effort to divert his attention that we bought the hamster. Christine would sit in his huge hands and run up and down his arms. Father could hear her scampering around in her cage doing tricks on her wheel at night while Mother was asleep. She was a much-loved pet, a huge success with the whole family and very good-natured. She never tried to remove anyone's finger, as far as I can recall, not even when woken from a deep sleep with a gentle prod.

Now, as we know all too well, hamsters have short lives and one day Christine was looking listless, sleepy and very fat. 'There is nothing I can do,' said the vet. 'She's got a kind of animal dropsy. The best thing is to put her to sleep.'

After much protestation from me he said he would try to delay this terrible event and gave me some pills, tiny ones like children's hundreds-and-thousands.

'Shall I bring her back next week?' I asked.

'If she's alive,' the vet said bleakly.

Feeding pills to a reluctant hamster is no easy task. John and I took it in turns giving Christine the required dose at four-hourly intervals throughout the night. After we had each completed our delicate task we set the alarm for the other to do the next dose. I have a photograph of my brother-in-law holding Christine while John tries to coax her to take her tablet. Inevitably I have to report that the vet was right. Christine was buried with full honours in the front garden at Burton Road.

Some might say it was an eccentric family that Shirley was about the join, but she never showed any sign of losing her nerve. Indeed she went out one day and bought a three-piece suite, a two-seater settee and two country-style chairs, in the sales in Brixton. I knew then that our wedding day was not far away.

11

Closing Down

When John left school in March 1959, the month of his 16th birthday, I think everyone agreed it would be a disaster if he got too heavily involved in the family business, which was becoming a burden to us all. Father hadn't wanted me to join the firm either but I, in my obstinacy, had paid no attention. Of course John, like the rest of us, had helped out from the age of nine, as soon as he could usefully shovel sand and cement, but we all recognised that in John's case the most important thing was to complete his O-level exams in the summer and get some kind of job qualifications for his future career.

One reason why John left before his O-levels was so that he could help at home. In fact John did help out at the workshop part-time for a while. I have a photograph taken in the front garden of Burton Road in the latter half of 1959, of John dressed in dusty work clothes with some of the ornaments we had just finished. Because we couldn't back a lorry into the yard of our workshop (luckily the van could make it), complete lorry loads of sand were dumped in the street and then we had to shovel it over a seven-foot wall. John was very good at this, and at mixing cement. Both jobs were quicker with the two of us working together. I enjoyed this time because it gave me the opportunity to work with John. I had missed a lot of his upbringing while in Coldharbour Lane because most domestic matters were dealt with by Mother and Pat. I usually arrived home tired out after long hours spent in the workshop and

Mother would only tell me about the things she thought important enough to need my attention. Now I found that working with my brother was fun, for he was an energetic young man who more than pulled his weight. Yet he was capable of having a laugh.

My diary for 24 June 1959 (in which I wrote down an order for two large cats) says John applied for his first job on that day – I think as a clerk at Price Forbes, the City insurance brokers. There is an often repeated story that John applied for a job as a bus conductor but was turned down in favour of a cheerful black lady because he couldn't add up the fares quickly enough. This is rubbish – he was actually rejected because of his height – he is six foot. Most people don't realise how tall he is. London buses are just not designed for conductors as tall as John, as was later confirmed for me by my father-in-law who worked for London Transport as an instructor of bus conductors.

During this time we all became well acquainted with Brixton Market and were on first-name terms with many of the stallholders. I found it very irritating, when John visited the market for his film about Brixton during the last General Election campaign, to hear the media say it was contrived. For John it has always been the most natural thing in the world to talk to traders and customers in Brixton Market, sometimes on personal terms, sometimes as a councillor on his soap box.

I well remember Christmas Eve 1959 when John, aged 16, and I were looking around the market for last-minute bargains to buy with the little money we had. It was getting late and we were on our way home when I noticed that the stallholder on the corner by Brixton Road was dumping Christmas trees on a pile of rubbish. We hadn't had a Christmas tree in our house for many years, and now I could see a seven-foot tree apparently going begging. When I asked the man if he was throwing it away he looked at me as if I were an idiot and said he was keeping it there until next year. If ever he needed an assistant, I thought, it wouldn't be me. But eventually I wore him down – he was packing up and anxious to go home, so he said I could take it.

I called John, who was by now further down the road and reluctant to get involved. 'We can't take that,' he said, giving me a disapproving look as I struggled with the tree. I soon persuaded him to take the thin end while I took the thick end and we set off past the police station back to Burton Road. It was our first Christmas in our own home for some years and I still have two photographs to remind me of that tree. One shows John holding the family dog, while the other is of the dark-haired beauty who by the following Christmas was to be my wife. The tree was much appreciated by all, the more so for being free.

John was always very keen on music in his teenage years in Burton Road. He used to record Top of the Pops on a Philips reel-to-reel recorder which used to change hands between us, depending who was in funds at the time. In those days we recorded through a microphone rather than through a direct lead, so there was always the problem of what to do with Mother's budgie. This was a musical bird which would sing along with the music when John was trying to record. He tried covering the cage with a cloth and moving it to another room, but most of John's recordings still ended up with an additional unwanted artist on them. John's attempts at recording were finally curtailed when he became interested in politics and more and more Young Conservatives were calling at Burton Road.

The new year started badly for Major's Garden Ornaments and failed to improve. With each week it became more of a struggle, and we knew something had to be done. Worn moulds, which we couldn't afford to replace, meant that I had to carve many of the figures into shape afterwards. There was a shortage of benches in the workshop, so that I had to put the full moulds on the floor to set, then pick them up again to remove the cast. We only had gas light and Tilly lamps, and there was no proper heating system, which was a serious problem when there was a heavy frost. It all added to the workload and reduced the time available to go out and look for new customers, which was now my responsibility, because Mother was no longer well enough to do it.

The van and the motorcycle had gone, because we were unable to keep up with the payments. The van had been scarcely roadworthy, with its kingpins badly worn, and it was probably cheaper to use outside transport for deliveries than to pay the tax and insurance. But its loss was a blow to my self-esteem, and I felt I had let Father down. As for the motorbike, this was just a way of keeping up with my friend Ted who was forever buying bigger bikes. Now I was back to pedal power, although this wasn't a great hardship because I had no time anyway for motorbike trips.

Without an injection of further capital the situation was hopeless. I wanted to get married to a lovely girl who fortunately put love before money and was prepared to take me, broke as I was. But to be truthful I was now 28 and tired of fighting and getting nowhere. It was time to quit before I was too old to start a fresh career. John was 17 by now and seemed old enough to look after his own future.

We wrote to all our main customers, including Mr Spiers, Commander David and Bentalls and told them we were closing down for good. Mr Spiers wrote back beseeching us to keep going. He promised to increase his orders and advances and said he would love to buy the business off us if he wasn't so tied up with his own shop in Cliftonville in Kent. Then came a generous offer from Commander David of David's Rural Industries, a kind of garden centre. He said he would clear all our debts, invest in new moulds and equipment and take me on as manager, paying me a good wage. Although I had almost made up my mind to start a new career, this seemed like an offer we couldn't refuse. We wouldn't have the profit, but nor would we have the worry. For the first time since Woolworths I would have a steady wage. So Major's Garden Ornaments became David's Garden Ornaments.

All of a sudden we had electric light and a gas ring for making the tea. Although I had to do everything myself, which was quite hard work, I was given money to buy good strong timber and make much-needed new benches. I was given time to make new moulds and provided with sand, cement, new shovels, watering cans, brooms, shellac, paint and stone dust for the finishing process.

To complete the luxury I soon had a van at my disposal, with a driver/helper called Ernie. My new colleague was quite a character and provided me with many comic turns. He once cut in front of a London bus, clipping its wing and somehow convinced the bus-driver it was his (the bus-driver's) fault. Roughly every fourth time out he would return with part of the van in the back – a bumper, a wing-mirror or some other inconseqential piece of equipment that had just fallen off, entirely by itself according to Ernie, who never admitted guilt.

Ernie had a stutter, usually only a slight one, but it became quite acute when he was worried or excited. So whenever the van was involved in one of these incidents of minor metal-fatigue it took considerable patience, on the part of himself and his listener, to try to unravel exactly what had happened. I was thankful that I didn't own the van, and Commander David, who was a kindly man, never said a word to Ernie except 'Be careful.' Although not the world's greatest driver, Ernie was a lovable character. Commander David would occasionally ask me to keep an eye on the van, and this of course I did – strange though it may seem, the van never came to any harm when it was parked in the yard. When Ernie brought it back from one of his hair-raising assault courses we just had to patch it up for another day and put the damage down to fate.

Commander David was a very generous employer and I always had the impression that he bought Major's Garden Ornaments more to help us out of our difficulties rather than to make a profit. This had its downside because what we really needed was to expand into a more commercially viable operation. The Commander's son, who was a barrister, said his father was a bit too soft on some of his suppliers, notably the people who made his wattle fences. He would pay them in advance and then be surprised, when he went to chase them up, that they weren't in. 'I know what happens,' Commander David's son told me. 'The word goes out to head for the hills, Commander David is coming. They ignore all his messages. I'm afraid they take him for a mug.' One lesson I learned from working for him is never to mistake a man's good nature for stupidity. I always had an enormous respect for him. He paid me good wages and overtime rates and let me get on with my job. I often earned overtime packing orders for Mr Spiers, who remained a regular customer but could only come up to London when his Cliftonville shop was closed on Sundays.

The only other recruit at this time was my brother John. He was out of work and fed up with alternating between job-searching and going to the pictures. He used to go to the little cinema, now the Ritzy, near Woolworths where Shirley worked. It was a very happy time for me, working with my brother for an employer I liked and respected. John and I both had bicycles and would cycle to work early, dropping in on a café later for a little breakfast when funds allowed. Sometimes John and I went home at lunchtime, for he was a growing lad and needed his food – at six foot he was actually an inch taller than me, but he was becoming quite muscular. On these occasions we would risk our necks travelling back to Burton Road in the van with Ernie.

One morning John and I arrived for work to find that the yard gates had been badly smashed, probably by a lorry reversing into them while turning in the road in the night. We had to report the damage to Commander David, as owner of the firm, and wait for the repairs to be done. In the meantime John and I shored up the gates from the inside, nailing the beams to keep the yard secure because the cast-iron hinges were broken. The problem was that we couldn't use the gate and had to climb a seven-foot wall to get in and out of the yard. John was six foot and I was five foot eleven, so we could reach the top of the wall and pull ourselves up, but sometimes we startled passers-by. There was a large pile of sand on the inside, which softened the impact on the way in and made the climb much easier on the way out.

On one occasion we were both sitting astride the wall contemplating the jump down onto the sand. I felt some hot smelly breath on the back of my neck. Then I heard a voice from above, which is not what you expect when you are on top of a seven-foot wall. It makes you feel rather apprehensive and vulnerable.

'What's going on?' said the voice.

John and I looked round sharply and found ourselves staring into the eyes of a very large horse. It bared its teeth, nodded its head and appeared to be laughing at us. At this point we burst into laughter ourselves. I'm sorry to say this made a very unfavourable impression on the mounted policeman who was sitting on the horse and becoming more serious by the second. 'Hello, hello,' he said, as policemen do when maintaining their composure. One of us said that the horse had approached so quietly that it must have been wearing carpet slippers, but this didn't alleviate the situation as far as the policeman was concerned. It was some time before we were able to regain a straight face and explain to his satisfaction about the gates. How I wish the people who say John is a grey man could have seen him then. If they had, they wouldn't say anything like that again.

When in funds we took it in turns to go to the baker's in the next street and buy a cake each for our morning break. The day of our other brush with the police John had gone to the baker's – a quick run up the sand pile, on top of the wall, then thump, as he jumped down the other side. The next thing I expected to see, after a short interval, was two nice cakes on top of the wall, with John's hands pulling him up from the other side. Instead he was gone for a long time. Then I heard a strange voice outside followed by a banging on the gates which, of course, wouldn't open.

Climbing up the sand pile I looked over the wall to see John and a rather stony-faced plain-clothes police officer.

'This young man says he works here,' said the policeman, 'but he jumped over the wall and ran up the road.'

I explained that I was the manager of the firm, that the gates were broken, that it was our tea break and that he was wasting our precious tea time. 'He is my current bun-fetcher,' I said wittily, but the officer failed to smile.

I spared the officer no details, but he seemed unconvinced, probably because I looked as disreputable as John did. Then he noticed our matching cement-stained clothing and realised we were genuine. He let John resume his mission to the baker's but looked disappointed that he had missed the opportunity of an easy arrest and a chance to go back to the police station for a cup of tea.

One night at about 10.30 I was walking back to the workshop, having been home for a meal and half an hour's rest, when I saw some policemen stopping people by the cinema on the corner of Coldharbour Lane and Denmark Hill. I was carrying a zip-up bag containing paint brushes, tins of paint, a bottle of turps and some pieces of cut glass which made a clinking noise as I walked along. I tried not to look suspicious as two officers approached, one old and bored, the other young and keen.

'Hello, sir,' said the young one in his best policeman's voice. 'And where are we going at this time of night then?'

'I'm on my way to paint the animals' eyes and the ducks' beaks, officer,' I said, looking him straight in the eye. 'Oh, and the crocodiles' teeth.'

The older policeman was quite amused by this. He decided I

wasn't as mad as I seemed but he wanted to hear what his young colleague would ask next.

'And what have we in the bag then, sir?' he persisted, eventually telling me to open it up.

There was a look of humiliation on the young officer's face when he saw that my explanation was true. As I walked off, still clinking, the older one said, 'Bloody fool.' Whether he was referring to his colleague or to me I don't know, but the hard-pressed police in Brixton today must wish they encountered a few more people as innocent as me.

12

Married Life

Once the garden ornaments business had been sold to Commander David, with me staying on as its principal employee, I had a regular wage again and was able to plan our wedding. I told Shirley that if we saved for another year we could have a white wedding, but she had had enough waiting and chose to get married immediately in a register office. Shirley agreed that, although I would no longer be living in Burton Road, I would go on paying my mother a weekly payment each week for as long as she needed it. In fact we planned to rent the top floor of Shirley's parents' house as a flat. I started painting and laying carpets while Shirley began paying weekly instalments for some furniture at Smart's.

So we were married on 3 September 1960, with Ted as best man and Mother and Pat organising the catering at Burton Road. We didn't have enough money for a proper reception or indeed for a honeymoon, although Commander David had given me an extra week off.

The night before the wedding I had an alarming backlog of ducks and gnomes to paint and I worked until four in the morning, although I managed to get home for an hour to see my bride, who was spending the evening in Burton Road. I have a photograph of both of us taken by John on that occasion as a kind of reassurance for Shirley that I was there and wouldn't be working all night. Little did she know that I went back to the workshop later and had less than four hours' sleep, getting up at eight for a haircut in Camberwell. It seemed important to get these ornaments out of the way in case they ruined our honeymoon.

I made it to the register office on time and we only had a short wait while the registrar finished the previous wedding. Now it was our turn. All went well until we arrived at the point where Shirley was supposed to confirm her willingness to take me for her husband. Suddenly she burst into torrents of tears. I know it isn't unusual for brides or their mothers to cry gently at weddings but Shirley was really sobbing. Was it relief, I wondered, or was it despair? The registrar looked at me and raised his eyebrows. I looked at Shirley, then back at the registrar and raised my eyebrows. He raised his eyebrows at the witnesses, and they all raised theirs in reply. It was almost as if eyebrows were a key part of the ceremony. Then he looked at Shirley and said: 'Are you sure you wish to marry?' To my eternal gratitude she then stopped crying and said, 'Yes.'

Shirley's widowed aunt Rose had solved the problem of the honeymoon by lending us a chalet on the Isle of Sheppey, which is probably not everyone's ideal holiday location but honeymooning beggars can't be choosers. After our first night in our new home in Margate Road in Brixton we set off next morning for the chalet Arcadia. The bus from Sheerness dropped us about a mile short of our destination and we trudged with our suitcases through fields of cows and pigs who were to be our companions on our first week of married life. I still have a china pig, given me by Shirley, as a memento of this challenging time.

Aunt Rose, it later emerged, hadn't been to the chalet Arcadia for several years. It was perched not on a rocky outcrop as I thought, but near the edge of a mud cliff which had receded alarmingly since she had last seen it. It was dusty and badly in need of paint and had a musty interior. Shirley, who had golden memories of childhood holidays there many years previously, was as disappointed as I was.

'Where's the bathroom?' I asked Shirley.

'Over the other side of the camp,' she replied.

When it came to communal bathrooms, I had a touch of the snob about me – perhaps I still have – and on this occasion it showed on my face. Shirley looked sad, and as she sat on the edge of the bed she caught her stocking on something and it ran into a huge ladder.

'I'm sorry,' she said, bursting into tears. 'It's a mess. We'll go home.'

'Don't worry, we'll soon fix it,' I said as I sat down on the bed beside Shirley and put my arm around her. 'It only needs a clean-up and an airing.'

As I looked at her little face, tear-stained and screwed up, I felt like the biggest cad in the world not providing her with a proper honeymoon. Once more she said we'd better go home, but what chance did we have, I thought, if we allowed a little set-back like this to defeat us right at the start?

'Come on, let's get started,' I said. 'We'll soon be cosy. We'll get some heat on first.'

Shirley said there was a big gas cylinder outside but when we looked at it we found it was empty. I went to the camp shop and a man wheeled another one over and connected it, a huge one, three months' supply, he said. So much for our free week's holiday, I thought, as I paid for it. Meanwhile Shirley had been sweeping and cleaning, and a couple of hours later when the chalet had warmed up things looked much better. We had a very happy holiday, taking the ferry across the Thames estuary to Southend, then staying late and returning on the last boat, which was rather small and worried Shirley a little. We toured the island, and I made my first visit to an eel-and-pie shop in Leysdon. We visited the church and spent hours talking to the pigs. I remember our honeymoon with nostalgia and sometimes get out the photographs to remind us of it.

Living in our one-bedroom flat in Margate Road, I came to know my parents-in-law very well. They lived just beneath us. Shirley's father, William Wilson, worked on the buses as a Blue Badge, a conductor instructor. Her mother Milly was lovely, kind-hearted, small, with dark hair, somewhat scatty. Whenever you were in trouble she would be there to help. She could always raise a laugh, usually without intending to. Many were the times I would explain something in great detail apparently with her full attention, only to discover that she hadn't a clue what I was talking about. 'When will you ever learn?' Shirley would say to me later.

As a couple they were very close, and an example to the pair of us as we started out on married life. Theirs was an old-fashioned relationship – he would sometimes call from his armchair for his newspaper which was on a table nearby. They were to die within two months of each other nearly twenty years later. First Milly, then her husband, broken-hearted without his Milly.

A year after we married we all moved to Thornton Heath Pond near Croydon, sharing a house as before with Shirley's parents downstairs and us upstairs. I always thought of them more as parents than in-laws. After five years Fiona was born, followed by Mark two years later in 1967, and this is where a close family is invaluable. Shirley and I both had jobs, and her parents would take the children to and from school and look after them until we came home. The children were so devoted to their grandparents that even when we were at home they would often spend their time downstairs with them rather than upstairs with us. It was a situation which many hard-pressed working parents would envy.

As I was still working in the Camberwell workshop I was able to visit my parents most days in Burton Road, and Shirley did too when she was working in Woolworths. She would go at lunchtimes for a gourmet fry-up provided by John.

Father was by now in sad decline, and he eventually died in 1962, aged 82. I had been called to his bedside in Burton Road by

Mother and was with him most of the last night, as were the rest of the family, but I was asleep in another room at the moment he died. Although he wasn't conscious, I had a feeling of guilt that I wasn't holding his hand when he died, especially as I felt I had let him down by not keeping the family business going. Both John and Pat have tried to reassure me that I did as much as anyone could have done, but I still wonder. John has said that without Pat's and my efforts to preserve family stability, he wouldn't be where he is today, although I am inclined to think he would have made it somehow, whatever the odds.

Although he had been very frail, Father's death was a terrible shock. The Variety Artists Benevolent Fund, who had given him a small pension, paid for his funeral in Streatham. My mother and Pat and her husband Peter continued to live in Burton Road until 1966, when they all moved to Thornton Heath Pond so as to unite the family.

It was in September 1962 that David's Rural Industries closed down, taking the garden ornaments business with it once and for all (although Mr Spiers bought all the moulds). It was now clear that I would have to find another way of making a living, as my father and my old headmaster had told me all along, whether I liked it or not. I had seen an advertisement for someone wanting to learn plastic moulding. It looked quite interesting to me, partly because I liked the idea of making something and partly because it had a shift system, which meant I could work nights two weeks a month and see the children in the daytime.

Interesting, however, it was not. It was one of those industrial scenes you associate with Victorian times. My job was to make plastic bottle caps using a manual press. There were about seven different sizes of bottle caps. This might have contributed a little variety, but in fact it only added to the tedium, because it involved finding different pellets of raw plastic powder and then dropping them into the mould with a special loading board. There was

123

another board for removing the moulded caps, which then had to be turned out onto a table and sorted into separate bins. It was monotonous work – frustrating, infuriating and very smelly.

Doing this for ten hours a night was enough to drive anyone mad, but it was made worse by the fact that there was only one other man in the factory at night, and he often got the hump (probably with good reason) and was in such a filthy temper that he didn't speak to me for the entire week.

The pay was poor and they docked an hour if you were more than three minutes late. There was a special bonus for producing a particular kind of measuring cap, but this was so difficult to make that the bonus was almost impossible to achieve. To work fast you had to roll up your sleeves. This meant you burned your arms. By the time I got home in the morning Shirley would have left for work and my mother-in-law provided me with hot soup before I went to bed. It was my doctor who advised me that he couldn't guarantee my physical or mental health if I continued with this, so I gave it up after six months.

From here I went to the South Eastern Electricity Board, known as Seeboard. I had never worked in electricity before, but I read a massive book on the subject before I went for the interview, and this apparently did the trick. On my first day the shop steward from the ETU told me I would have to join the union. I have never had anything against trade unions, but I do believe in freedom of choice. I was furious and very nearly resigned, but Shirley wisely restrained me, saying I should join the union and only resign if they forced me to do something against my will.

I was now a Meter Fixer, paired with an Installation Inspector called Jeff with whom I was to spend many happy years until he became foreman of the department. Jeff was a very pleasant man and I got on with him well. We would often go to his house for tea when we had a break. He was one of the top inspectors and he taught me a lot. He reminded me of Father, demanding my best work.

One day I wasn't feeling at all well and Jeff was having to do half my work as well as his own – in fact I ended up just passing him screwdrivers and other tools. At lunchtime he told me I should go home, but I said I'd stick it out because I might feel better later. That night I was quite ill and Shirley insisted I see the doctor next day. He sent me to the Mayday Hospital, where acute appendicitis was diagnosed. My last words in the operating theatre, the nurse later told me, were: 'Tell them my time sheet is in the pocket of the van.'

I may have had a reputation for being accident-prone at Seeboard. Once I stuck a screwdriver in my eye and came away from the Mayday Hospital with my entire head in bandages. I also slipped down some icy steps, twisting my back and losing the contents of my tool-bag in deep snow. But probably my worst accident was when a kindly lady crept up behind me as I was working on her meter and, putting her hand on my shoulder, asked if I would like a cup of tea. This knocked me off balance and as I tried to save myself I put my hand on the open cut-out. I was thrown back against the opposite wall with a splat, sliding down the wall, dazed like a cartoon character with stars before my eyes.

'Yes, I'd love a cup of tea,' I told the lady, who was now looking very worried. 'Do you mind if I have it sitting down here?'

13

Butlins

One day Shirley came home from work at Philips with an idea for a holiday. 'Terry, how about going to Butlins at Bognor?' she said. 'Charlie from work is taking his family. A holiday will do you good and the children will love it.'

I wasn't at all keen. For one thing, I didn't know Charlie, or his family. For another, I had had enough of wash-houses and cook houses in the army. But Shirley began to explain that Butlins wasn't like that any more. 'They have their own bathrooms and toilets', she said, 'and self-catering chalets'. She must have been very persuasive, because I agreed to give it a try.

Charlie, who was later to become my supervisor at Philips when I joined the firm, brought some friends, so we had three chalets between twelve of us, including Mark and Fiona and my niece Mandy. Each chalet had a double bedroom for the parents and divan beds for the children in the living-room, and of course that essential bathroom.

Before the first week was out I was suggesting to Shirley that we should book for the following year. I was very impressed by the amenities in Blue Camp where we stayed the first time. It was close to an indoor swimming pool, an outdoor swimming pool, a sports field and a large boating lake. There was a launderette, a nursery, a putting green and a sheltered garden where you could sit and read, and woods nearby where you could photograph the squirrels. There were newsagents, fish-and-chip shops, ice-cream shops, cafés, a self-service diner, a food supermarket and places where you could buy shoes and clothes.

You could play snooker, table tennis, darts or even indoor bowls. There were sports contests, ballroom-dancing competitions and a donkey derby, free rides on the funfair and penny machines in the amusement arcade, plus bars and bookies. The theatre showed a feature film in the afternoon and a live show at night, and there was a separate children's theatre. I may have forgotten something, but it seemed to me there was something here for everyone. Alternatively there was Bognor, only ten minutes' walk away.

The main reason I was hooked was the Variety Shows, something I had missed for more than twenty years, since we lived in Worcester Park. Thanks probably to television, there are very few places where you can see a good live revue or variety show these days. But the self-catering chalets were also a major factor. I am often asked why I haven't been more adventurous with my holidays over the years, but the truth is that although I like going places I also like to be back in my own home at night. Self-catering seems to offer the best of both worlds – after you have settled down the chalet almost feels like home.

The standard chalets were rather basic when we first went to Butlins in 1975, but they were a lot more comfortable than army barracks, which is what I had expected. As neither of us drives a car, Bognor was also very convenient, just a direct train ride from Croydon, followed by a short taxi trip, or even a walk, to the camp. At one time the Butlins Redcoats met every train at Bognor, with a bus for the guests and a lorry to take their suitcases to the camp, but these days the Redcoats have been made redundant in this department because it seems that practically everyone except us travels by car.

I am often asked how we can bear to go to Butlins with all those loudspeakers and wake-up calls, and my reply always is that these are things of the past. If you are on a catering tariff you have to get up so that the chalet maids can clean the chalet and make the beds, but if you are on a self-catering holiday you can stay in bed as long as you like.

One year they made a mistake and booked us into Yellow Camp instead of Blue Camp. Conservative as always, I wasn't happy about this change at first, but later I came to prefer this side of the camp, although it was further away from the theatre. Shirley was the one who eventually began to tire of this routine, so I had a chat one morning over a cup of coffee with my good friend the senior accommodation manager. He suggested a new concept, the County Suite, which had two bedrooms and a separate lounge area, a tiled bathroom with electric shower, fitted kitchen, hall cupboard and a colour television. It was newly decorated, nice and shiny and clean, and Shirley was soon hooked, if only to please me. As an added attraction it was in the County Suite that Shirley discovered Cross Wits, which was to become her favourite TV quiz game, which we always watch if we can after breakfast. Sometimes I think I have been unfair, always taking my wife to the same place on holiday. One day, perhaps, we shall go on a cruise.

At first we took one week at Butlins. Then we made it two or three, one in June and another one or sometimes two in September. In fifteen years between 1975 and 1990 we missed only three years at Butlins, 1980-1982, first because Shirley's parents were very ill and then because we lost a lot of money moving house. The *Daily Mirror* seemed to think it very funny when I said we couldn't afford our annual visit to Butlins in 1991, the year after John became Prime Minister, and sent a reporter to talk to me about this. I was trying to make a serious point, which I had learned from my parents, who very seldom took a holiday, that at times of financial hardship the first thing that goes out of the window is the family holiday. The *Mirror* was much more interested in the fact that I spent my time in Bognor photographing squirrels, after a chance remark I made to the photographer while complimenting him on his zoom lens. The *Sunday Express* took me to Butlins for the day, which I enjoyed at the time partly because I thought it would give them a chance to put the record straight and say what an excellent place it is. But as so often happens, Terry was being taken for a ride: the piece they published was a frivolous one.

I have seen many changes in entertainment and accommodation at the Bognor Centre, some more welcome than others. I didn't approve of moving the film from the evening to the afternoon, because not all of us want to spend all our evenings in bars and night clubs, especially if we have children. I have nothing against the Aquasplash water world or the shopping plaza with trendy eateries, but I think I preferred the Regency Building, with its old-time dancing and wrestling, which was there until 1985.

The Regency Building contained an indoor swimming pool with glass sides, where the excellent coach Bob Price taught both my children to swim. Mr Price, later Entertainments Manager and after that a leading light of the Aquasplash, taught Mark from scratch in one week and turned Fiona from a doggy paddler to a swimmer after years of school lessons had failed. As a non-swimmer myself I have always felt my children should learn to swim, and this alone makes Butlins worthwhile.

Some changes were superficial. The Blinking Owl suddenly became the Village Inn, with medieval banquets every Thursday. The Princes Ballroom, where I've watched my children play for hours, became the Ocean Ballroom, and the York Building, with its games room, was transformed into the Sports Complex. Blue Camp became Barnam Village, Red Camp Ructon Village, Yellow Camp Yapton Village, and Westergate Village sprang up in the corner of the coach park. The Pig and Whistle revue bar became the Manhattan, with an improved stage for marvellous cabaret acts.

We saw Mike Read have the audiences in stitches in the Manhattan. He's a bit blue for for my taste, but he has the excuse that

130

he's genuinely funny, unlike most blue comedians. We also saw Tommy Trinder in the Butlins Theatre. He had the audience eating out of his hand, and the more he was heckled the funnier he became. There have been many occasions when Shirley and I have been at home watching the same old faces on television wondering why we couldn't see some of the great shows we see at Butlins. Sometimes well-known TV names appear at Butlins, but as a rule there are a lot of very good acts there which never get the television spot they deserve.

Talking to people about our holidays at Butlins I am often astounded by their view of such places and their ignorance of the facilities available. Many of the people who turn their noses up at these true holiday centres through lack of information would thoroughly enjoy them if they had the chance.

Journalists who have talked to me about Butlins are always surprised that I'm not a competition-minded sing-along sort of person. They don't seem to realise that you can choose the type of holiday you want, whether quiet or boisterous. I like a quiet but active holiday, whereas Shirley prefers a lazier one. Perhaps lazy isn't quite the right word, but there's no doubt that she likes to lie in the sun when it's available, while I prefer to wander round the camp looking at the shops or going into Bognor itself. Both of us like to visit the market in Chichester and make a couple of visits to Hotham Park nearby. This is a lovely park, sadly damaged by the two big storms but rapidly recovering its old beauty. Once in the park Shirley and I just wander around in peace and quiet, or sometimes Shirley sits and reads while I creep around the trees, with my camera at the ready, trying to get a good photograph of the squirrels or ducks.

I shall never forget the year when I twisted my back on the day Shirley had her fractured ankle out of plaster. It was just a week before we were due to go on holiday. Both of us spent the next week determined not to miss Butlins. Putting heavy cases on the luggage rack of the train didn't improve matters, and on the first evening, at the end of the show, I tried to get up from my seat but just couldn't move. It took Shirley and two Redcoats to get me on my feet, and it was slow progress up the aisle grasping the backs of the seats.

When, after several days, there was no improvement Shirley suggested we go home. Certainly not, I protested, we had come for a holiday, and a holiday we were going to have. Next day I visited Boots in Bognor, who gave me some painkillers, warning me that this wouldn't cure the problem – I would have to see a doctor. We had worked hard for this holiday, I told the chemist, and the doctor would have to wait. We got some funny looks that week – Shirley with a weak leg in support bandages and me bent double on her arm, while she had to pull me to my feet again every time we sat down. We couldn't play indoor bowls, but we didn't miss a show. It turned out to be one of our best holidays at Butlins, perhaps because we were both in such a mess that we had to work at keeping each other happy. Maybe there's a moral here, that a holiday is like a marriage. You have to work at it to get the best out of it.

Perhaps one day someone will write an up-to-date history of Butlins. It will be filled with nostalgia for millions of people for whom Billy Butlin's dream came true, while for those who haven't experienced it for themselves it will dispel a few prejudices and misapprehensions. It will be a fascinating chronicle of the 20th-century leisure industry, a book well worth reading.

14

John and the Media

About a month after Fiona's first birthday in November 1966 John went to work in West Africa for the Standard Chartered Bank, but about six months later he smashed his leg very badly in a car crash. Mother received a letter from the bank saying they were flying him home.

John was sent to the Mayday Hospital near Croydon, where so many of the family have spent time over the years. I used to visit him there, and so did Shirley who was by then pregnant with our son Mark. John was in fair spirits, considering his leg, but a little restless. His only complaint was that he couldn't hear music of the type he liked. First the headphone plug was faulty and then, when it was fixed, he found that he only had access to certain programmes. So Shirley and I decided to buy him a portable radio with an earphone so that he could listen in private.

I remember this radio well. It was a Bush T R 130, well made and covered with black leather. It cost £15-19-5 plus 10/6 for the earpiece – I still have the receipt. It was such a success that I bought another one, in brown, for myself. Equipped with his radio and a pile of books, John became a model patient, but I noticed that he spent most of his time reading. I have often thought this period of learning and reflection may well have been a turning point in his life.

When he was discharged from the Mayday John spent much of his convalescence with Pat, Peter and their daughter and Mother at Thornton Heath before having further treatment at Kings College Hospital. This return to the family fold wasn't a great success because Mother, who of course lived with Pat, fussed too much over her injured son, who was now after all an independently-minded adult who had worked in the City and in Africa. The general bustle of the house, with people constantly dropping in to see Mother, was also probably too much for him, especially as his bad leg left him with no easy means of escape. But there was also a practical problem. Because he couldn't bend his leg, he couldn't get to the upstairs lavatory, and if he used the outside loo his outstretched leg prevented the door from closing. So he went and finished his convalescence in a quieter place with friends.

Mother's chest problems were getting worse and she was spending more and more time in the Mayday Hospital: always the same complaint, always the same ward. She had become a popular figure in Thornton Heath, and my brother-in-law Peter, a tool-maker by trade, who was a keen handyman as well as a tolerant son-in-law, decided to make a gate in the fence into the alley at the bottom of the garden to make things easier for her many friends who dropped by. There was an Asian lady called Mrs Shaw who came up through the new garden gate into the house for a chat every time she went to the shops and then stopped for another gossip on the way home again. Mother had made friends with two of the nurses from the Mayday, and they often spent the entire day in Pat's house when off duty as they preferred it to the nurses' home at the hospital.

As a child, the death of my mother was something I always feared. I had persuaded myself, in conversations with my teddy bear, that the bear and I would be allowed to accompany her on her journey to heaven to quell my anxiety about separation. By the time she did eventually die, in September 1970, the bear had predeceased her and I at 38 was approaching middle age. I wasn't at the Mayday Hospital when she died, and it was a terrible shock to lose her, and to see her join my father at the Variety Artists Benevolent Fund Chapel in Streatham. The local shop where she bought her cigarettes and sweets closed its doors on the day of the funeral until the hearse had left, despite a long queue of customers outside.

Mother's death came at a difficult time for John and Norma who were planning to get married in October. John's political career was now well under way. He had narrowly won Ferndale Ward in the Tory landslide of 1968, and he became Vice Chairman of Brixton Conservative Association the following year and Chairman in 1970. One of his close friends and political colleagues, Clive Jones, often came with him to visit Mother, and he came to her funeral.

Norma had been on the scene a relatively short time, compared with my own courtship with Shirley, but she went with John to see Mother in the Mayday Hospital. When Mother died John suggested postponing the wedding. It was Pat who persuaded him that the last thing Mother would have wanted was to delay this happy day.

It was a busy time for Norma's mother, who organised the wedding. Norma made her own dress, the bridesmaids' dresses and the pageboys' outfit. Norma being Norma, everything was done exactly right, as it always was. Our daughter Fiona was one of the bridesmaids, as was Pat's daughter Mandy, and the leader of the trio was Norma's cousin Claire. Our son Mark was supposed to be a pageboy, but he was very young and refused to perform on the day. Norma had the bridesmaids in shoes that matched their dresses, and this put Shirley on the spot because she had decided on a navy-and-green outfit. Where was she to find the shoes to go with this? Well, this is where Terry comes in handy – busy with a paintbrush just as I had been, for different reasons, on my own wedding day. It was a lovely wedding, with Norma's friend June Bronhill singing during the service and a reception afterwards at

Brixton Town Hall. It has been sad to see some papers saying that John's family didn't go to his wedding. Mother and Father had died, of course, but the rest of us were all there. Pat hates being photographed but was certainly at the church and at the reception. Her daughter Mandy is in the photos, as are all my family, but her son Christopher hadn't yet been born.

Less than eighteen months later we had another family shock when Pat's husband Peter died, leaving her with two very young children, Mandy and Christopher. It is a tribute to her skills as a mother that she managed to bring them up as a single parent and that she is now a grandmother herself. As in any close family, John and I have always tried to help her in our different ways.

In my case, I was keen to complete the various DIY projects Peter had already started in his house, finishing a cupboard in a disused fireplace, building a giant mantelpiece which continued as shelves in the alcoves on either side. He had a strange collection of small planks of different lengths and thicknesses, which meant that I had to do hours of laborious planing and dowelling to get the sizes I required. Then I re-wired the house because Pat needed a new lighting system. I used to go to her house after work, and by the time I got home Shirley was usually in bed. My own family hardly saw me for months. Sadly, before I had finished my work on Pat's house, she had to sell it and move to a smaller one.

When my parents-in-law died we moved from the house where we had all lived together, largely because we felt the time had come to start a new life. The housing association who agreed to buy the house pulled out at the last minute after we had already done the deal on our new house in Wallington near Philips in Croydon, where Shirley and I were both by now working. I quickly found a private buyer but had to drop £10,000, which left us practically broke. After I had been there fifteen years Philips closed down my section of the firm, Philips Service, leaving me redundant along with nearly everyone else. I was left with only a small pension. In

my last two years at Philips I was off work half the time because of
an old back problem and had spent several weeks lying on the floor.
I returned to work several times, only to be sent back to my doctor
by the firm's medical centre as unfit to work. All this and my age
(now nearly 60) made it almost impossible for me to find a suitable
position when Philips Service closed. Well, at least Shirley and I
have each other, and I think we can say we have earned everything
we have.

John and Norma moved to Beckenham in 1973, and then to
Hemmingford Grey in 1977 after he had been adopted as Conservative Candidate for Huntingdon. They had now moved in
completely the opposite direction from us, in practically every
sense, but I'm glad to say we've always kept in close touch.

Ever since John became Prime Minister, and indeed since he
became Chancellor, I have been asked some fairly silly questions
about him by the media. My brother and sister and I all have a
strong sense of family loyalty inherited from our parents, so of
course we always like to defend each other. I genuinely think he is
an excellent leader of his party and of the country. It is annoying
sometimes to be asked whether he knows what he wants or where
he's going, because I happen to know he always has. John has
formed his main ideas over a period of many years, and they are
not fleeting fancies of the moment, though how quickly he can
implement them may depend on the amount of co-operation he
gets. He has always known where he's going and I'm not at all
surprised that he is Prime Minister.

He is also very tough. My family has been through some rough
times, and each of us, in our different ways, is very resilient.
Sometimes people who are brought up in a harsh environment
have learned to avoid confrontation, but it is a mistake to assume,
just because he doesn't seem abrasive, that John is a pushover, as
anyone who thinks so will soon discover. All of us were brought up
in a loving environment, so no one could ever say we are emotion-

ally deprived, as many politically ambitious families are. We were taught by Father, perhaps because of his experience in the theatre or maybe because of his American upbringing, to treat everyone we meet as equally important. This is not the traditional route to political power, but there are many people who find it very refreshing.

I am also asked about Norma, a lovely and intelligent girl whom I've always been fond of. Having first adjusted to being a mother and living in the country, she has now adapted to her difficult new role very well. It is the first time for 30 years that a Tory Prime Minister has had a wife, so she has had no one to turn to for advice. I think she studied the role very carefully and now carries it out to perfection. She is not one of those people who rush headlong into things without consideration. Some people may have thought she was a little out of her depth to start with – that was perfectly natural, after all – but I haven't heard that criticism recently. I'm often asked how she felt when John became Prime Minister, but I'm not hedging when I say I don't know. It's not the sort of question I would ask her. If anyone wants to know they should ask Norma, not me.

I am also asked what I think of Mrs Thatcher, and I have to say I have always admired her, even when her policies led to Philips making redundancies and me losing my job in 1989. I have met the lady only twice, once at No 11, and once in the Chancellor's office in the House. She was very polite to me, only correcting me when I referred to the 'Poll Tax'. She told me 'Community Charge' was the correct term but appeared not to take any offence.

The question I hate being asked is why Lady Thatcher has been saying less than helpful things recently. For many years I was one of her most enthusiastic supporters and I remained one even towards the end of her time, when with many others I began to think she was losing her touch and was disregarding the people who voted for her. Many of the people I worked with were beginning to say that she had to go, that we needed someone more in tune with our way of thinking. After John was made Chancellor the stick I had to take about her increased. I became an obvious target for remarks by many people in the office where I worked who were fed up with her ways. Whenever they said she must go, I stuck to my ground, saying: 'Look at all the great things she has done.' When they said she was arrogant and didn't care about ordinary people I had a stock reply. 'Oh yes, she does,' I would say with some authority. 'John tells me so.' I would relate little tales I had been told to illustrate the other, less cold, side to her nature – like the time a young lady serving dinner at Chequers tripped and deposited meat and gravy all over a minister and she went to comfort the girl, not the minister. I continued to support her, even after I was certain a change was needed, because I felt that, if an expert like John was prepared to support her, I should too. I just hoped she would stop looking for fights and get on with the job. After my firm closed and I found myself redundant, people would ask me: 'How can you support Thatcher when you're out of a job and can't get another?' 'Look abroad,' I would say – it was always the same answer. 'We're better off than a lot of countries. Things will come round in time. We've had all this before, and come out stronger.'

I was saying this right up to the time of the leadership challenge, despite my private thoughts. Why? Because I knew John was prepared to vote for her right up to the wire. How? Because of our conversations. As far as I'm aware, John only agreed to stand himself after he knew there was no hope for her. I have to admit I was hurt and mystified whenever I read of the criticism Margaret was reported to be making of John, the man we are told by the media whom she had chosen and supported as her successor and who had been so loyal to her.

I was especially hurt when I remembered how she complained about the treatment she received from her predecessor. Apparently she thinks her case is different because she never lost an election, whereas Ted Heath did. I find this reasoning odd, because John has never lost an election – in fact he won one against the odds. It is strange too that she has savaged former colleagues whom she chose for the Cabinet herself. What happened to her judgment then? Recently I heard her say on television that it was better to have them in the Cabinet then on the back benches making trouble. Why did I have a feeling of *déjà vu*?

Now that her memoirs have been published and she has had her say, perhaps her sadness at leaving office is passing and peace can reign. I hope those historians who were planning to say, as a footnote to her achievements, that she 'didn't know how to retire from office gracefully' will return their pens to their stands unused. Then I and many others can remember her great deeds while forgetting her miscalculations.

I'll even be prepared to say sorry for using the vulgar expression 'Poll Tax' to her face on that occasion when we met. She is a great and remarkable lady. I have also met Sir Denis and their son Mark at No 10, but not yet their daughter Carol. Carol is a plain-speaking young lady in a very similar position to my own. One day I hope I may meet her, for I have a sneaking feeling I might get on with her rather well.

A few months ago I was described as 'the Prime Minister's amazing brother' by the *Spectator* columnist Paul Johnson. I don't know why Mr Johnson is so easily amazed by me, never having spoken to me, but it may have something to do with the fact that he doesn't like my brother, or at least doesn't like him being Prime Minister. I believe that in his days as editor of the *New Statesman* a generation ago in the 1960s he used to hobnob with Harold Wilson in Downing Street, and latterly as a right-wing columnist he had the ear of Lady Thatcher at No 10. It must be terribly frustrating for Mr Johnson that time has moved on, so that we now have a Prime Minister who doesn't listen to him any more. After a lifetime of vacillation he must feel all washed up, rather as I did when the garden ornaments business collapsed. I was very grateful to a kind *Spectator* reader who came to my defence, writing a letter asking why he had to drag me into all this. I am only too glad to leave journalists alone, as long as they leave my family alone.

One night I turned on the television, intending to check the news on Teletext before going to bed, when I saw a newspaper columnist sounding off about my father being a 'failed trapeze artist'. It was a debate about the monarchy, and they were saying that if we had a republic the Queen might have to swear allegiance to the son of a failed trapeze artist.

This kind of remark gives me sleepless nights. It is deeply wounding when people try to discredit my parents in an effort to undermine John, though John himself is well able to take it. Family and honour are very important to me. Why should a journalist make a remark like this about my father without the slightest effort to check it? I know they haven't, because my sister Pat and I have all the information and no one ever asks us.

Next morning, still fuming, I rang my friend James Hughes-Onslow at the *Evening Standard*. I know I should be careful about calling a journalist a friend, but James is a friend, though he can be quite mischievous with stories he thinks are funny. After checking with Channel Four we found that the journalist who had insulted my father was Charles Moore, editor of the *Sunday Telegraph* and a well-known critic of John Major. James said he was at the same school as Mr Moore and gave me his home number, telling me to give him a hard time. He also got a diary reporter to call Mr Moore and demand a public explanation.

I missed Mr Moore but spoke to his wife, and she sounded such a charming lady that I was unable to voice my criticism of her husband. He later told the diary reporter that he 'didn't know my father was a successful trapeze artist'. This patronising remark made me even angrier than before, implying that, even if he was successful, Father was only a trapeze artist. The point I'm always trying to make is that Father did a lot of things in his life, some of them more successful than others, but the only thing which interests the media is that he did the trapeze. How would Charles Moore fare on the trapeze, I wonder, if he hadn't decided to pursue a more disreputable profession? Does he automatically assume that people are failures just because he doesn't know them to be a success? I can't imagine that he is a very successful newspaper editor if he doesn't check his facts.

The arrogance of some reporters takes the breath away, but there are many others with whom I get on very well. John McEntee of the *Sunday Express* has always treated me fairly, reporting what I have said, and not, as others do, what he wishes I had said. So when Mr McEntee asked if he could bring a photographer down on the night of the 1992 General Election I said he could, partly because, unlike most observers, I was confident of a good Tory victory. As soon as they arrived I could see that the photographer wasn't happy – the settee was in the wrong place in relation to the television set. With ten minutes to spare before the results started coming in they began to rearrange the living-room furniture and the wires connecting the video equipment. They chatted and snapped away, and then they left. I was in no mood to leave the telly, but waited until it was all over and savoured the last drops of victory. Then I had to put all the furniture and the video cables back in their right places next morning.

This was a pleasant enough interlude, but there are occasions when Shirley gets annoyed. Sometimes I waste a lot of time trying to be polite and helping reporters, only to find that they reward me with jokes at my family's expense, leaving me with nothing to show for my efforts but a large telephone bill. When John visited President Clinton for the first time, a reporter asked for an interview and then stayed for two hours getting a story that was never printed. Two hours, what a waste! I could have painted a door in that time.

Family and honour are the most important things in my life and this is as much due to the relative hardship of our years in Coldharbour Lane as to the more prosperous times we had before the war. Pat and I agree that that we have happy memories of that two-room flat in Brixton. This kind of upbringing gives you a very positive attitude to human nature, even when you know you are dealing with people of questionable character and background. We have often wondered what happened to the charmingly unpredictable Irish lads who had an eye on Pat? Did the lodger who was hauled off by the police for various misdemeanours relinquish his life of crime or move on to even greater wrongdoing? Wherever he is, I wish him well. Having lived in this situation one can contemplate these things without being censorious, as perhaps one might from a more comfortable vantage point.

The media are always trying to suggest that there are dark secrets in our family, but my own researches have been disappointing in this area. I have failed to discover any skeletons at all. The BBC's left-wing Panorama programme thought they were doing rather well before the last election when they said John was not a Lambeth resident and therefore not eligible to stand as a councillor when he was elected in 1968. If they had proved that the Prime Minister's career was based on a false start it would have been a good story, especially for Mr Kinnock, but unfortunately they were more interested in standing up the story than in establishing the truth. They asked the wrong questions and they got the wrong answers.

Panorama quoted Rose Oliphant, an old friend of Mother's who lived in Templar Street about 100 yards from Burton Road, saying that John didn't live in her house although he gave it as his address. In fact John lived in a flat just opposite, and because he had a communal front door and no telephone and was rarely in during the daytime Rose agreed to take all his messages and telephone calls, no small undertaking considering he was a busy councillor. This explanation was too boringly straightforward to merit the airtime Panorama gave to the original allegation.

Rose Oliphant, who has since died, was a pillar of the community in Myatt's Fields and secretary of the local garden society. She was terribly upset by this story. She rang me after Panorama had visited her, and she was in a very distressed state.

'Terry, I keep telling them my story is true but they keep coming back,' said Rose, a lovely lady who I don't think was capable of telling a lie. 'Last time I shut the door on them.'

She was so upset that I went to see her and told her not to worry about this stupid programme. It was the last time I saw her, for she died shortly afterwards.

15

A Leafy Suburb

Like many home owners, I suspect, we came to live where we do because it was the kind of place we could afford, not too far from where we used to live (therefore close to my sister) and convenient for work. I have to be careful when I say this because some members of the media have expressed surprise that the Prime Minister's brother can't afford anything better that Wallington, – a leafy south London suburb, as it has always seemed to me. (Perhaps they are afraid to admit that he is a man of the people.) Such condescending remarks are hurtful to my neighbours and myself, for we are proud of our homes and most of us try to keep them as nice as we can.

Like a lot of people these days, I do as much DIY work around the house as I can, which makes me a frequent visitor to the Texas store nearby. Shirley sometimes wishes I spent more time on DIY and less on researching my family history, although she understands that I only started on this project to defend the family against the misrepresentations of the media. There is a cupboard in the kitchen which took an age to construct because of various interruptions, mostly from members of the press. Recently, however, I surprised Shirley by starting and completing a bedside cabinet while she was at work one day.

As neither of us drives a car, being close to work was rather important, but Wallington has easy access by public transport to Croydon, London and the south coast. Fiona is the only one of us who has a car and often helps out with transport. She comes over once a week to take her mother to the supermarket and to help me when I have something heavy to collect.

Ours is a friendly little community. People talk to one another. You find you know most of the local people for some distance around, and we all keep an eye on one another. Our end of the street often reminds me of Worcester Park, where we were brought up. It is compact and amiable. There is lots of greenery although some trees have been cut down and replaced by saplings. The council has made the foolish mistake of replacing paving stones with tarmac, for reasons of economy we were told, but I say this is the path to mediocrity.

Both my immediate neighbours and luckily most of the locals knew me before my brother John became prominent in politics. They know I haven't changed and that I'm not given to putting on airs and graces, but quite a few like to talk about John and say how they think he's doing and give me messages for him.

It is a small terrace house and we have a small garden big enough to sit in but not too big to be a problem to look after. One bedroom is not much more than a box room with enough space for a bed and a wardrobe, so I may have to look for a larger house when I can. I sometimes think about the bungalow in Worcester Park, and my mind drifts back over the years to the times we had and all the things that happened there. Mr and Mrs Canter, the couple who purchased the bungalow from my father, recently moved. I'm sure that by the time they left they must have been fed-up with newspapers wanting to photograph the Prime Minister's old home.

The Canters are still friends of ours and they used to let me visit my old home several times. I was able to see things that brought back happy memories, the breeze-block wall I built, the front-garden wall made of blocks moulded by hand and some of my old pathway in the back garden. Sadly the fancy tile centre-piece, with leaf tiles I made by hand, in the front garden and the breeze-block

146

coal bunker are now gone. You can still see the place in the garage wall where I made a door so that the man next door could park his car in our garage. In a characteristically generous gesture my father decided that as the neighbour's car was new, while his own van was second-hand, the man next door should use our garage. But I had to extend it and build a special door.

I don't suppose Wallington is as nice now as it was years ago – there aren't so many trees – but that's the same everywhere, isn't it? All these places are so built up. Five of the top 40 London state schools listed in the *Evening Standard* magazine are in the area. We are also near Sutton, which has a very good shopping centre, theatre and library. Wallington is well provided with shops and Croydon's shopping centre is said to be the best in the south-east. We have sports centres and parks and good train and bus connections to Victoria, enabling you to enjoy London or take a train to anywhere in England. Call me unpretentious but I don't have any complaints about life in the suburbs near Croydon.

My waistline has suffered since I started researching and writing this book. An author's life is a sedentary one, compared with a garden ornament manufacturer's, and I don't think I've made the necessary adjustment to my diet. It's not that I eat very much when I'm sitting at my computer, but I do nibble away at snacks and I drink quite a lot of tea.

James Hughes-Onslow rang me one day from the *Evening Standard* to ask what I usually ate for breakfast. This, you might say, was none of his business, but he was doing an article about the British breakfast and, as he is a friend, I told him.

I'm like John, I'll eat anything. I'm very flexible about breakfast. It depends what I'm doing. I must admit, although it's not politically correct, that I do like bacon and eggs but I seldom have time. More often it's just cereal and maybe tea and toast. If I'm really in a hurry I leave the house without anything and may eat or drink nothing all day until quite late at night.

To be quick with a cooked breakfast I put the bacon in the microwave, which is healthier than frying it. Sometimes I cook the egg in the microwave as well, usually cracking it into a saucer rather than a plate because it makes the egg smaller but thicker. The egg comes out of the microwave looking like a fried egg but tasting like a poached egg. Then you add a handsome dab of Lea & Perrins or Heinz and you have a breakfast fit for a king. You have to prick the yolk of the egg to prevent it exploding. Shirley sometimes used to forget this, with spectacular results.

The truth is that for most of my life food has taken second place to work. If I am busy and interested in what I am doing I tend to forget about meals. Sometimes I eat nothing all day. It's only when I get bored, or reach a temporary impasse, that I stop and think about food. If people come in and Shirley makes coffee, I'll have some of that, but if I'm left to my own devices I'll have a cup of tea. The one thing Shirley found a little strange when we first married was my penchant for a cooked supper, a hangover from my teenage years when I would come in from the workshops at about nine o'clock, have a wash and then join my parents for a meal. Father and Mother had got used to having a cooked meal late at night during their days on the stage, when they would eat after the show sometimes as late as midnight. It took Shirley some time to wean me off this habit and I'm not sure she has been entirely successful.

Sometimes at Colindale I eat sausages and chips in a café which I recommend near the underground, but there was one day last year when I missed breakfast because I was rushing for the train, and then I missed lunch because I was busy in the library. I had to stop at Downing Street to deliver something on my way home in the evening (I have to switch from the tube to the train anyway at Victoria, which is a short walk from Whitehall), and by that time I was tired, hungry and thirsty. There was a long queue filing past a desk, and a lady asked me if I was there for the reception. Norma

148

was hosting a reception event for a cancer charity, and after delivering my package I went upstairs to see if I might have a few moments to chat with Norma.

At the reception I found some very interesting, well-informed and charming people to talk to, and a waitress who provided me with orange juice. 'Would you like a drink, Mr Major?' she said in a soft voice. The first drink made me realise how thirsty I was, not having had anything to drink all day, and I had several glasses, one each time she came round with the tray, probably about four altogether. It was then that I saw a waitress I had met before. She knew I only drank orange juice and when I reached out for another glass she turned the tray away from me. 'I'll get get you an orange juice, Mr Major,' she said. 'Those are Bucks Fizz.'

I left Downing Street for Victoria at about 9.30 and caught my train for East Croydon. Thanks to the warmth of the train I soon felt very sleepy, but not inebriated as some people would no doubt like to believe. In no time I nodded off, and the next thing I knew was that a man was tapping me on the shoulder telling me I was at Gatwick. It was cold and wet at the station and getting late, so by way of killing time before the next train back to Croydon I went to have a look at the air terminal.

Next day I was telling James how absurd it was that at the age of 60 I had never flown in an aircraft. 'Do you know, James,' I said. 'It's the first time I've ever been to an aerodrome.'

James said he had never heard anyone say such a thing before and asked if he could quote me in the *Evening Standard*.

A reporter later rang and I told him I hoped to fly somewhere sometime 'even if it's only to Manchester'.

This prompted an article in a Manchester evening paper asking what I had got against Manchester.

'Nothing,' I demurred. 'I love Manchester. My father was born near Manchester. I only mentioned it because it was the first short-haul flight that came to mind.'

Granada Television wanted to fly me to their Manchester studio so that I could elaborate on my thoughts on that beautiful city, which my brother was backing at the time for the Olympic Games, on their morning show. The prospect of such an interview made me much more nervous than my first flight would have done and I turned down the offer. Meanwhile Lynn Barber of the *Independent on Sunday* had picked up my comments on flying. This paper said it would take me to on a day trip to Paris, and a man who operated sight-seeing flights over Norfolk offered to fly me in a bi-plane.

James said I should think of somewhere I really wanted to go, and he would try to arrange it through the *Evening Standard*. He suggested going to America because of my father's childhood there.

I could see the media angle. There is the Prime Minister buzzing around the world addressing the world's problems while his elder brother Terry has never been abroad except on National Service. It is a tribute to James's powers of persuasion that he managed to convince me that an innocent trip abroad needn't be embarrassing to me or my brother. He told me he was in no position to make fun of me because he had never been to New York himself, and had only once crossed the Atlantic, travelling as a member of the crew on a cargo ship to Newfoundland 30 years ago. Eventually I agreed, but persuading Shirley was more difficult, in fact impossible. She said boats yes, but planes no, and wouldn't be budged.

I very nearly lost my nerve and cancelled the trip a few weeks beforehand when I visited Zippo's Circus in south London. Because of my father's connection I love both variety shows and the circus, and am glad to do anything to promote the art. They had asked me to present certificates to circus trainees who had just completed a course. I was most impressed by these young people, as I told the assembled press. Six months earlier they hadn't been higher than a step ladder but now they were performing forty feet up a rope. Next day all the tabloids published silly pictures of me (taken when I wasn't ready) falling off a unicycle while being supported by some scantily dressed young artists. Mr Pepys in the *Evening Standard* suggested that the Tory party should put me under wraps to save the Prime Minister from further embarrassment. I was rather cross about his remarks, but James was unperturbed.

'Don't worry,' he said. 'I doubt whether anyone pays much attention to Mr Pepys.'

Another paper annoyed me by suggesting that John had helped rush a passport through for me. This was totally untrue. In fact, although I am known as Terry Major-Ball, my surname is given as Ball in my birth certificate while my christian names are Terry Major. As my brother John Major is given as my next of kin this caused some confusion and I had to get a letter from him to confirm my identity.

I became a little worried about travel insurance after reading about a woman who went to America and was found face down in her hotel swimming pool. She was pronounced dead on arrival, but though the hospital could do nothing for her they still charged the family £6,000 for medical services, of which the insurance paid up only £3,000. I would have hated to do this to Shirley, but James assured me this was all taken care of.

By way of a joke he said: 'You can swim anyway, can't you, Terry?'

I answered that I couldn't and had no intention of going anywhere near a swimming pool.

Shirley and Fiona said clothes were half the price in America and provided me with a shopping list complete with measurements, Fiona giving very exact instructions on the colour and style of jeans. Small things began to worry me – are you allowed camera batteries on the aircraft, would the film have to travel separately because of X-rays, did my electric razor require an adaptor, would there be someone to prevent me sleeping on the flight because I have always been a terrible snorer? And so on.

I bought a new suitcase, thinking ours were too big, only to discover that Shirley kept the small ones inside the big ones. I also wanted to buy some new shoes. James urged me not to, saying that new shoes were always a disaster on holiday, but I went ahead and bought two pairs of Clark's finest casuals and wore one pair all day at Colindale. Next day I told James I could see the wisdom of what he had said. However I persisted and they were comfortable by the time we went. All went well in New York until on the last day a lady in high heels trod on my foot and the swelling made them tight again.

By the time the Virgin Atlantic limo arrived ouside my house, I was all ready. I even had time to go to the corner shop and get some boiled sweets for the flight, as Fiona had advised.

16

New York

As a young man I often wanted to go to Heathrow. My friend Ted, who was a bit of a wanderer, used to suggest going there in his car, but somehow we never made it. Now here I was on my first visit to this great airport and I hardly had a chance to look at it. I don't suppose not seeing enough of the airport is a common complaint among the millions of passengers who queue for hours at various terminals, but the Virgin Atlantic limousine which picked me up in Wallington sped through at such speed that I couldn't take it all in. I think I may have to go back and have another look one day.

In no time James and I were in the capable hands of some extremely attractive young ladies, and I was having to apologise to them for addressing them as such. I have no doubt that it is politically incorrect to refer to airline staff in this way, but I did explain that I came from an old theatrical family and this was quite normal in those circles. One of the air stewardesses bore a striking resemblance to Mother, and when I told her this she became even more charming. All the formalities, such as tickets and passports which must be such a worry to most travellers, were efficiently dealt with by these smiling ladies without causing me any concern and, as I told them, I was beginning to realise why Shirley hadn't let me out of her sight for more than a full day in 33 years of marriage. I mightn't be able to trust myself with all those beautiful females. 'Now I see how attractive you all are I can see why my wife Shirley keeps me in sight,' I told them by way of explaining why I could

153

only be in New York for three days. 'That's as long as I would want to be away from my wife. There hasn't been a day in 33 years of marriage that I haven't seen her.'

In the Virgin Upper Class departure lounge there were more young ladies, this time offering drinks and hand massage. I went for a cup of tea and a manicure and received a short lecture on the state of my hands. It was probably the result of many years making garden ornaments, I explained, sometimes mixing the cement with bare hands in freezing temperatures. She made me give a solemn undertaking that I would look after my hands in future and would not do this kind of work again. She was doing such a thorough job that when the flight was called she hadn't quite finished and had to arrange a further instalment with the in-flight manicurist. I joked with these young ladies that I would be ready to shake hands with anyone in New York.

On the aeroplane we were offered drinks, and although I usually only take orange juice, as I have explained, I thought this was a suitable occasion to celebrate with Champagne. I began to joke with the cabin staff that it would take a hell of a lot of rubber bands to get this machine off the ground and that I was quite surprised they had room for any passengers. The inside of the first-class compartment looked remarkably like the InterCity trains I have seen at Victoria Station, spacious and comfortable-looking, not that I have ever been on an InterCity train – yet.

Flying for the first time, I fully expected it to be a frightening experience, but I suppose one is affected by the docile calm of the other passengers. Air travellers, at least first-class ones, seem totally untouched by the excitement of travel. Most of them were reading newspapers as the colossal machine gathered speed down the runway. Did they know what was going on out there, I began to wonder.

Unlike all the other passengers I was amazed when we cleared the end of the runway. 'Beautiful,' was all I could say. 'Incredible.'

There was a slight inclination of the angle of the floor and, as if in a spectacular circus trick, we were climbing at an amazing speed. I was astonished how smooth it was. The suburbs of south London, which I knew so well, were like toy town with dinky cars scuttling around. In no time we were above the clouds looking down on a powdery antarctic landscape. It looked as if you could walk on it. Glancing around the rest of the compartment, I could see that for my fellow travellers this was an everyday occurrence, but for me it was a remarkable experience. I was also very impressed by all the gadgetry that came out of the arms of the seats – the television set, the table, the lights and radio controls.

Although it was strange, there was something reassuringly familiar. It was a bit like sitting in an armchair at home, watching the telly and having my food brought to me on a tray (though I don't really expect this kind of treatment from my wife), the big difference being that I didn't have to worry about doing the washing up afterwards, or boiling the kettle and getting the tea. The service was marvellous, especially when you see the tiny kitchen. The piece of cod I had melted in the mouth, and the sauce was delicious. I thought of the deck passengers on the SS Indiana who, Father had told me, were fed with salted herrings from a barrel when he crossed the Atlantic in the 1880s.

Because the Virgin staff knew it was my first flight I was invited to the cockpit to meet the captain. I congratulated him on his smooth take-off, but he told me smooth take-offs were relatively easy. Smooth landings were always much more difficult, he explained, and there would be some nasty cross winds at Newark when we arrived. This is a fine thing to say, 30,000 feet above Greenland on a stormy night in November, to someone who has experienced one take-off but no landings, but by now I realised I was in capable hands and had absolute confidence in all the Virgin staff. If I had seen the captain again after we landed I would have congratulated him once more. It seemed a very smooth landing to me, although James told me that it had startled the other travel-weary passengers, who had been clinging to their armrests with whitening knuckles.

At Newark Airport there was another of Mr Richard Branson's charming young ladies waiting at the door of the aircraft with an immigration official to take us off first and escort us through customs to another waiting limo. I couldn't have been better treated if I had been Prime Minister. I still hadn't encountered the queues other air travellers encounter.

By the time we arrived at the Westbury Hotel in Madison Avenue, where I had a suite with flowers and bowls of fruit and a magnificent view of the Manhattan skyline, I was beginning to think I could handle the pace of John's jet set life after all. It was rather less hassle that that journey from Colindale to Croydon, when I ended up at Gatwick. Mind you, thanks to the wonders of transport technology, there was very little evidence to convince me that I had actually crossed the Atlantic at all. Perhaps we were, after all, in the Westbury Hotel in London.

Next morning I realised we were on foreign territory when my electric razor wouldn't work. It was one of the problems of going abroad I had been warned about, and indeed I had anticipated it, saying to Shirley that I was worried about my adaptor. When a simple everyday thing like this goes wrong you begin to think everything is going to go wrong and that the whole operation will end in disaster. It was a gloomy Terry who rang James in his room at 6.30 (not such an unreasonable hour as it sounds because of the five-hour time difference) to say I would be out looking for a new razor as soon as the shops were open. The prospect of me wandering the streets of Manhattan alone clearly alarmed James, who offered to lend me a conventional razor and suggested I should ring Room Service.

The hotel engineer was baffled, so I dismantled the razor adaptor myself using a nail file. I tightened a loose screw, and when

I put it together again it worked. 'My years with the electricity board have paid dividends at last,' I told James. It was a small triumph, but I began to feel I was more in control. When James said I should ask Room Service to bring my breakfast to my room, I had to say I wasn't used to this kind of treatment. Being in control means I like to go downstairs and get my own breakfast. As far as possible I like to look after myself – I suppose this is why I like the self-catering at Butlins.

We arranged to meet at 8.00 downstairs in the Polo Lounge – a well-known meeting place for Manhattan tycoons to have breakfast discussions, we were soon to discover. American businessmen are much more direct with one another than British ones. They don't pretend that breakfast is a social occasion, and they don't spare each other any paperwork or technical detail required to pull off a deal. 'Yes, yes, I know that,' one man at the next table said to another as they tried to clarify a point. 'That's what we're doing here, for Christ's sake.'

James was late coming down for breakfast because he was on the telephone to various friends trying to arrange our itinerary. James is always on the telephone, I now realise. Although he said he had never been to New York before, it sometimes seemed to me that half the population of Manhattan had been at school with him. I don't know how many schools James went to, but he bumped into at least four old boys quite casually in Madison Avenue alone. One of them, a reporter with the *Sunday Telegraph* called Mark Palmer, was so startled he thought he was involved in a frame-up.

While I was waiting, I talked to the hotel concierge, who came from Liverpool. He told me he knew Wallington, which was reassuring. I also spoke with a man sitting at the next table who turned out to be an Irish film producer. When James came down to breakfast it transpired that he knew this man – yes, he was at school with him, in Dublin. When the film producer started to talk about a friend he had played golf with the previous weekend in England, James knew him too – he was at school with him, near Slough.

James said we had three lunch appointments for that day, and when we came out of breakfast there were two people waiting for us in the foyer. One was the *Evening Standard*'s photographer Ken Towner, over in the Big Apple for the New York Fashion Show, who wanted pictures of me eating a bagel, reading the *New York Times*, negotiating with a cab driver, walking in Central Park, among typical New York scenes. The other was Alexander Chancellor, former editor of the *Spectator* and now columnist on the *New Yorker*, who accompanied us on this walkabout providing an entertaining commentary. Ken went back to his fashion show after he had finished, but I am grateful to Alexander for telling me quite a lot about New York over the next few days, taking us to the *New Yorker* offices, to Joe Allen's restaurant, to see *Guys and Dolls* on Broadway, to Grand Central station, the Chrysler building and several of the magnificent Manhattan banks.

James and Alexander became a little exasperated with me at times for stopping and talking at great length with passers-by. Apparently New Yorkers are not known for their friendliness with strangers, but this wasn't my experience. Everyone I spoke to was extremely friendly. I had a long conversation with some cops, as the Americans call them, outside Grand Central station. We discussed why they carried guns whereas British ones didn't. I looked under their jackets at their radios and batons, and they didn't mind at all. They told me that not all American police stations are as chaotic as they seem in films. I can't understand why New York cops are thought to be aggressive. They seem friendly enough to me.

Similarly I found New York cabbies were nearly always obliging, and I had a long talk with some men down a manhole fixing the electrics. They were very interested to know how the underground electrical system works in Croydon. One lady I stopped for directions asked me back to her appartment to see a typical New York home. James thinks I must have a high boredom threshold talking to all these people, but how are you supposed to find out what New York is like if you don't talk to strangers? We can't all walk up and down Madison Avenue all day chatting to old boys we were at school with. I like to think that people should talk to one another more, not less, and that this is a lesson some people in public life could learn. Usually if you adopt a down-to-earth approach you find there are others who will respond.

Lunch on our first day was with a lady from Dallas called Linda Lambert who happens to be a Friend of the Metropolitan Museum. She gave us lunch in the glass-covered top-floor dining room which has a spectacular view of Central Park. She pointed out an enormous 60-seat table and chairs made by Lord Linley who had just been to the Metropolitan himself that week with his new bride. Seeing Rodin's *Burghers of Calais*, I was prompted to recall my own modest efforts to capture the human form while making garden ornaments. It is far easier to build up a figure in plaster or cement than to carve it from wood or marble. Seeing some of those half-finished marble figures by Michelangelo sometimes gives me nightmares – the fear of nearly reaching perfection and then chipping off a vital organ at the last minute.

I also worry about the astronomical price of art these days, compared with ordinary pictures you or I would want to have in our living-rooms. Of course I can appreciate the beauty of a Van Gogh sunflower, but is it really worth £20 million? Is it that different from a sunflower picture you might buy in a gallery in Croydon? I do not hesitate to give my views when I visit the Prime Minister's apartment in Downing Street where there are several paintings on loan from the National Gallery, and when I read about the sale of a painting for an astronomical sum. The Metropolitan is perhaps the most beautiful museum I have ever seen, but whenever I go to a place like this these things do worry me.

I do not know whether Father ever saw a Broadway musical, but I think they were probably well after his time in America. He would certainly have enjoyed *Guys and Dolls* at the Martin Beck Theatre. This was a very professional production, far better than anything I've seen in London, and I was particularly impressed by the lively performance of Faith Prince as Miss Adelaide. I'm sure we'll be hearing more of her. But I thought the theatre itself was a little tacky, not up to the standard of London's West End or even of some London suburban theatres.

Afterwards we went to Joe Allen's, where most of the customers were transfixed by the New York mayoral election results on telly. Then Alexander noticed that the lady at the next table was Liza Minnelli. I could see from the way James was fumbling for his camera under the table that he regarded this as a photo-opportunity, but Alexander and I were trying to restrain him, saying how would he like it if people photographed him in restaurants. He said he didn't know, he could only ask and began to shuffle his chair towards her.

James is an accomplished name-dropper when the situation demands, and he started off with a preamble about how he had been at Liza's sister Lorna Luft's wedding in London in 1976 (probably more as a newshound than as a guest). Then he said that I was John Major's brother and my father had been an international figure in the music-hall era who greatly admired her mother. I could see Miss Minnelli looking at me and noting without much enthusiasm that I did indeed resemble my brother. Then at the end of her meal she came over and spoke to me. I expressed my own admiration for her and Father's for Judy Garland. James had by now been shamed into putting his camera away, but I rather wish he hadn't. A picture of me and Liza Minnelli would have improved my street cred.

16. New York

Next morning James organised a helicopter trip around Manhattan. I wasn't too keen at first because those films of Superman flying among the skyscrapers are frightening enough. Also, I thought you had to wear a crash helmet to go in a helicopter, and I've always found them claustrophobic. I've tended to avoid jobs on building sites which require hard hats and have completely given up motorcycles since crash helmets became compulsory. Well, I have to say the experience was far from claustrophobic. I felt like a bird darting in around the Statue of Liberty, the World Trade Centre and the Empire State Building. It wasn't at all frightening and I could have stayed up there all day. I was surprised to find that the Statue of Liberty was green, caused by atmospheric corrosion, and I suppose this shows that I've been watching some very old films.

Later at Alexander's offices at the *New Yorker* I had a brief glimpse of their editor-in-chief Tina Brown. I was describing my helicopter experience to various staff writers when Tina Brown suddenly stopped in her tracks thinking she had seen the Prime Minister. When it was explained that I was actually John's brother she said 'One sees some strange things in the corridor these days.'

'I hope that's not supposed to be a disparaging remark, young lady,' I exclaimed as she disappeared back into her office.

While in this part of town I took the chance to visit the New York City Library to see if I could find any trace of my father's stay in America. Staff were very patient as I told them the whole story about the SS Indiana, the Carnegie Steelworks, the house in the foothills of the Allegheny Mountains and the Girard military scholarship, and about John being Prime Minister, but James was flagging a little, having heard it so many times before.

'That's very interesting, Mr Major,' said the lady at the information desk, directing us to someone else.

After meeting three or four different people, we worked our way up to the third floor, to the genealogy department, and then to the microfilm room. We found a reference to the Girard scholarship which Father had mentioned, and we found a picture of the SS Indiana. We looked through the lists of several hundred names of people called Ball who lived near Pittsburgh between 1880 and 1900, but James was becoming restless and hungry. I pointed out that I sometimes sat in a library all day without anything to eat and without discovering any facts at all.

'I can see you aren't cut out for this kind of work,' I told him frostily.

James had two more chance encounters, both in Madison Avenue, which provided delightful interludes in our stay. First we met his godfather, Sir John Borthwick, who said he usually lived in Bermuda but had come to New York to buy a new golf club, a no. 1 wood, and practise his swing. He asked us to lunch in the Knickerbocker Club in Fifth Avenue, a magnificently elegant gentleman's club where James pointed out the distinguished biographer Kenneth Rose and where we were given Maryland crab cakes and acorn soup. I haven't been able to persuade Shirley that I would eat such delicacies at home if only I could get hold of them.

Our other meeting was with the millionaire novelist and art critic Andrew Solomon whom James had met in London the week before. Expressing the usual astonishment to see us, Andrew said he was on his way to a cocktail party in Fifth Avenue and why didn't we come along? This has never happened to me in London, but I suppose New York is different. Certainly the party was quite unlike anything I had experienced at home, and I wasn't at all sure whether to take them seriously, or whether they took me seriously. It was in a penthouse with a sensational view down Fifth Avenue and across Central Park and full of paintings I'd be reluctant to pay for even if I could afford them.

One young Wall Street banker was terribly concerned that I had never flown in an aircraft before.

'Do you have a phobia of flying, or are you just worried about jet-lag?' he asked.

I told him the difficulties my family had encountered when the garden ornament business collapsed after the war had prevented travel, and that my wife Shirley and I had never had any need to travel any further than from Croydon to Margate.

They listened to me attentively and courteously, but I wasn't at all sure whether they were being serious later in the evening when, perhaps fortified by dry martinis, they began to suggest that Britain should be a republic.

I had an audience of about ten as I tried to explain that in my days in the army it was considered essential to have the Queen as a figurehead and commander-in-chief. Britain was very different from the United States, I told them.

I think they were just having a bit of fun teasing me, a sort of odd party trick. I certainly enjoyed arguing with them.

One of the guests was a man called Claus von Bulow, whom I had never heard of before but, having heard about him, I'm not sure I'd count him as a family friend. He told me he had met John at cricket matches at Getty's ground at Wormsley and at his box at Lord's. 'I suppose you're very keen on cricket, too,' he said.

'Not really,' I said, 'John's the sporty one of the family. I had little time for sport when I was younger.'

Later some of us adjourned to a new restaurant called La Goulou in Madison Avenue. There was an extremely blonde divorcee who sat beside me and paid close attention to me all evening.

'Glamorous blondes will hold no terrors for me now,' I told James across the table. 'I'll be telling Shirley all about this one.'

All in all I think my first trip across the Atlantic was a great success. After my initial apprehension I would have liked to have stayed much longer. I met Sir David Steel at Newark airport on the way home, and when I told him it was the first time in 33 years I had ever been separated from my wife for more than 24 hours he said I should try not to make it too often.

If I ever go travelling again I'd want to take my wife. It was an astonishing experience, probably the most exciting thing I've ever done. It gave me a new respect for my father and for John, people who have seen the world and know more about it than I do. It made me wonder what I've been doing, staying in one corner of England all my life. I could happily have stayed for a fortnight. My only worry is that Virgin Atlantic and the Westbury Hotel treated me so well that if I ever go anywhere again it is bound to be an anti-climax. The next time I saw John I told him about my experiences and he listened politely and with genuine interest.

Then he said, 'Sorry, Terry, I must go now. I'm due at a meeting, in the Cabinet Room.'

As he left his flat to go downstairs, I thought once again how very little time for relaxation there is in the busy life of a Prime Minister.

Index